THE
STAFFORDSHIRE
BULL TERRIER

Dr Dieter Fleig

RINGPRESS

ISBN 1 86054 149 6

Printed and bound in Singapore
by Kyodo Printing Co

10 9 8 7 6 5 4 3 2 1

AUTHOR'S NOTE

Why write a book about the Staffordshire Bull Terrier?

There is no other breed in the whole world whose popularity has increased at such a rate since its relatively late recognition in the early 1930s. For example, by 1987 in Britain – the foremost dog-breeding country – Staffords had the ninth highest number of registrations of all breeds. Out of twenty-four terrier breeds Staffords were number one, the most popular terrier in Britain. This popularity has continued to rise.

It has not been so easy for the breed to attract the right owners in other European countries – few people realise that within its small, muscular, compact body is a very lovable personality. This dog, with its powerful head, is an all-purpose dog, a sort of everybody's Man Friday. *The Staffordshire Bull Terrier Today* is intended to reveal not only the physical attributes of the breed but also the merits of its temperament.

The so-called 'fighting dogs' receive considerable adverse publicity from the media. Ignorance among animal welfare organisations, governments and politicians has made the general public uncertain of the real nature of the 'fighting dog'. Those who read this book will discover that the Stafford has a unique character with an abundant love of people, including children. In today's world a Stafford can be the ideal, adaptable companion for many dog lovers. It is psychologically disturbed people who can make a dog into a mental cripple and a fighting machine: they do not need the best-looking dog, nor even a particular breed, for this purpose.

In England, Pitbulls are banned by the Dangerous Dogs' Act; on the continent, nearly every country has its own 'dangerous dogs' and the Staffordshire Bull Terrier is involved in many press campaigns and new legislation. We are working very hard to protect these breeds – some countries have already banned the import and breeding of some breeds, and the dogs which are already in the country must be muzzled and kept on a leash in public areas.

Most dramatic for the owners is that all the press campaigns and new laws are favouring the anti-dog lobby. It is getting more and more difficult to explain to neighbours or landlords that these so-called 'fighting dogs' are so charming – they love people, and are no danger at all. If there are any problems with dogs, it is because of the owners who abuse them and who do not educate them properly.

This book was first published in 1988 in Germany and its success was surprising. It is actually the first book about Staffords originally written in German, and its main purpose was to show German, Austrian and Swiss dog lovers what a great breed the Stafford is.

On my visits to England I heard from many Stafford enthusiasts who were disappointed that they could not read the German edition. Considering the old saying that there is little sense carrying coals to Newcastle, I was surprised and pleased that there was evident demand from English Stafford fanciers for a translation.

I was therefore grateful to Boydell & Brewer for publishing a book by a German author about an English breed, and to Mr and Mrs Feiken-Preuss in Germany, the sponsors of the original German edition. I am now delighted that Ringpress Books have decided to publish this revised, updated edition.

I hope I have given English-speaking readers a true picture of the Staffordshire; it will certainly show the amount of work that needs to be undertaken in Europe to win new friends for the breed. I hope I have shown what a great dog the Stafford is: it must be protected from exploitation but at the same time it should be enjoyed for its wonderful character and adaptability – it is a dog with a very bright future.

I would like to record my gratitude to those people from whose books, articles and letters I have quoted. I owe a particular debt to Harry Taylor, editor of the *Black Country Bugle*, for permission to quote from his important features on Joe Mallen, published in the pages of the *Bugle*.

Dr Fleig

Rendorn Rule The Roust, bred by Norman and Dorothy Berry.

CONTENTS

The nature of puppies; Buying an older dog; Understanding puppy development; Trial periods for older dogs.

FOREWORD

Dr Fleig has written a most enlightening work on the breed: his observations are indeed an objective appraisal of the Stafford scene in Britain, and his book should satisfy both expert and novice.

The author, whose first love is the English Bull Terrier, or the Standard Bull Terrier as it is known on the Continent, has visited our shores many times. During these visits he has studied the Stafford intently, and become very knowledgeable about the breed and its history, as befits an academic of his stature. He is active in both breeds and must be considered one of the foremost authorities in Germany, where he is the warden for the regulation and pedigree control of the Stafford.

Norman Berry with a fine representative of Rendorn breeding.

Early chapters present an outline of the history of the breed, briefly discussing the blood sports and pastimes of former days, which naturally Dr Fleig abhors and condemns. He also gives an insight into the lives of the old Black Country people, their interest in the Stafford, and their involvement in its development.

Readers will enjoy the stories and anecdotes about some great characters, particularly Joe Mallen and the other notable people whose efforts laid the foundations and cornerstones of this great breed we all enjoy today; the book also includes some of Joe Mallen's theories, and his experiences during the formative years of the Staffordshire Bull Terrier Club.

Originally published in Germany by Dr Fleig's own publishing company, partly with a view to publicising the breed and educating the potential fancy in that country, this book is of great interest to Stafford enthusiasts throughout the world for its portrayal of the Stafford at shows and in less formal surroundings, where it excels as the greatest companion and friend any owner could wish for. This revised edition by Ringpress Books brings valuable knowledge about Staffordshire Bull Terriers to a new generation of owners.

Norman Berry 'Rendorn'

1 *HISTORY OF THE BREED*

A large exhibition was organised in 1974 in the Bear Gardens Museum in London by the Southern Counties Staffordshire Bull Terrier Club. This was not in order to celebrate the animal atrocities of the past, or to generate any interest in them. It was designed to explain how the anatomy and character of the present-day Stafford was dictated by its original purpose. The breed has its origins in the dog-fighting of the early 19th century and it is important to understand that dog-fighting at that time was hugely popular among certain sections of the population. But, of course, using animal fighting as a public spectacle goes back in time much further than that. Samuel Pepys recorded in his diary on August 14th 1666 that it was a "very rude and nasty pleasure".

The Romans had a method for appeasing exploited and oppressed people, 'panem et circenses' – bread and circuses. They served as a distraction from the miseries of life. In the Black Country, in the 19th century, people were mercilessly exploited. Not only were adults compelled to labour under terrible conditions in dangerous coalmines and ironworks for sixty hours or more a week, but it was quite usual for children to work ten hours a day underground. Hunger and poverty forced the whole family to pool their efforts in order to survive. In addition, they had few rights and little social standing. Those who know what affection from an animal can mean will appreciate why these despairing people kept pets – most of them dogs, who earned their own living as ratters and as guards.

THE ROAD TO RICHES

And dog-fighting? For such people dog-fighting could be of great importance. The dogs that defeated their opponents did not just earn their own keep: the owner of an accomplished fighter acquired prestige and esteem, as well as money. Betting on a good dog could earn more money than the poor owner would see for fourteen or sixteen hours' hard labour underground. Also, if one had a good dog and bred from it, then its offspring would also earn money.

Extreme poverty, poor health and hungry children suppressed any distaste people might have had for dog fights. In fact, the people themselves fared little better than their dogs. Recognition and success were not easily achieved, either at work or within the family, but were possible with a thriving and winning kennel. It is important to appreciate the social difficulties which lessened people's reservation towards brutality to understand why dog-fighting took place, how they could watch dogs fight, accept the role the dog must play in the fight, and apparently condone the recurring cruelty to animals.

Anyone who observes the bond between man and dog will agree that a complete understanding can develop between them. Man works for his own success, which brings him recognition in his own world. Likewise, the defeat of his dog become his defeat, but the victory – the dog's moment of glory – becomes his own triumph.

To understand the reasons behind bull-baiting, dog-fighting and cock-fighting, we need look no further than the depressed circumstances of the average working man in the 18th century; this is not to excuse it, but to explain it.

BULL-BAITING
It is not the aim of this book to describe blood sports in general, just those for which the ancestors of today's Stafford were systematically bred, but it is remarkable, when looking at old paintings and prints, how often dogs like the modern Stafford are portrayed. Is this only coincidence?

All breeds were originally bred for a certain purpose, and their physical appearance and nature are a consequence of this approach. I shall therefore outline briefly the original role of the Staffordshire Bull Terrier, which has shaped today's breed. Both man and dog were subjected to a severe selection process where the survivors were those who could fulfil the demands made upon them.

For bull-baiting, the fully-grown bull was tethered by a long rope to a bull-ring deeply embedded in the ground. It was the dog's job to seize the bull by its sensitive nose, to hang on and not let go at all costs. 'To pin the bull!' This was the goal.

Bull-baiting. A hand-coloured engraving by Henry Alken. London, c1820.

Considering the relative weight and strength of these animals, the dog's task is like that of David facing Goliath. The only dog that has a real chance of winning must be extremely careful, skilful, brave and tenacious. The dog's life was threatened not only by the pointed horns but also by the dangerous hooves of the steer. Many of the attackers were caught on the horns and flung high into the air. Often the horns pierced the flanks of the dogs, and many broke limbs and were crippled as a result of the fall back on to hard ground. During its attack, or if the dog fell, it could be trampled by the hooves. There were some very accomplished and experienced fighting steers specially bred and trained for this 'sport' and they killed hundreds of inexperienced dogs. Bulls developed their own fighting tactics by digging holes in the ground in which they could protect their sensitive noses, so that the fearful horns were all that awaited the attacking dog. Again and again, inexperienced owners risked the lives of their untried dogs in such fights.

The rules of the bullfight stated that only one dog at a time could be set on the bull. When the dog was injured and deemed unfit to fight further, a second, and later a third, would take its chance. Before an owner could test his dog's prowess he had to pay a stake which was forfeit to the owner if his dog should fail. Spectators would lay wagers for or against the bull; experienced gamblers who followed the progress of the animals would bet accordingly. Bullfights were an important social occasion and owners and spectators would be turned out in their Sunday best. A painting depicting such a scene in 1820 shows that the similarity between these dogs and the Staffords of the 1930s is striking.

The famous engraving *Bull Broke Loose* shows the popularity of bull-baiting events, which were likely to take on the nature of a public festival. Here again Stafford-like dogs are the main performers. The organisers of the bullfight charged a fee from each of the spectators; the wealthier ones sat in coaches, which were the equivalent of expensive seats or theatre boxes. In this picture, the bull's horns are blunted by leather balls, reducing the risk to the attacking dog. In this fight, the bull has managed to break loose and is wreaking its revenge on its two- and four-legged tormenters.

The old English Bulldog was also used for bull-baiting; it was a shorter-legged dog but exceptionally brave and clever. It would crawl flat on the ground towards its opponent, so as not to give the horns an easy target. The dog would wait and anticipate the right moment when it could attack its opponent's most vulnerable point, the bull's sensitive nose. Once the nose was seized, the dog had to hold on with an iron grip; if it were to let go it would be trampled to death by the hooves of its opponent. Such a task was definitely not easy and resulted in a ruthless weeding-out of the bulls' adversaries.

DOG-FIGHTING

Whether or not we want to hear about dog-fighting, the fact remains that the Staffordshire Bull Terrier was originally bred for dog-fighting. The preparations required for bull-baiting were much more elaborate, and a bull was not always available at the right time or place to test the gameness of the dogs. Normal social behaviour of wild dogs involves, to a marked degree, fighting among themselves. Fights take place to establish a hierarchy, a pecking order in the pack, and also to stake out territorial boundaries between packs. In such matters, fights play an important role. A fight between dogs would normally end with the overthrow of the weaker or unwilling opponent: the loser would display a gesture of humility and its submission would, under normal circumstances, end the fight. In dog-fighting, however, the fight had to be taken to the 'bitter end' and the dog's natural behaviour had to be altered by selective breeding over many generations. Breeding stock was chosen in which the killing instinct was dominant.

In the pit, dogs fought against dogs

of the same weight; for instance, a 10 kg dog would be matched against another of the same weight. No distinction was made between the sexes, so dogs fought the same and opposite sex on an equal basis. As with a boxing match, the fight consisted of a number of rounds. Instead of ropes surrounding a ring, the pit or fighting arena was built of firm boards. One of the rules of the fight was that if a dog let its opponent loose in one round, then in the next it must be the first to attack, otherwise it would be declared the loser. The attack was deemed valid only if the dog crossed the mid-line of the arena. Anyone who has seen a fight between dogs of the Bulldog type will appreciate the determination with which they will hang on and how difficult it can be to part them.

In the corners of the pit, the dogs were ministered to by their handlers and freshened up between rounds. Handlers were allowed to encourage their dogs verbally during the fight but not to come into direct contact with them. Yet, despite the intensity of the situation, the animals do not appear to attack the men. I believe the simple explanation is that these fighting dogs were bred to fight each other and not man. Without a direct effort to breed dogs that were friendly towards human beings, it would be impossible to control them for

fighting. This selective breeding resulted in a fighting dog with a nature that was compatible with man. This amiability towards man is still present, but unfortunately not enough people are aware of it.

Some of the fights could go on for hours, and they frequently ended with horrific injuries to both dogs, if not death. The winning dog, even if badly wounded, was the great hero, and the owner too became a success, financially and personally. Only dogs which were accomplished fighters were subsequently bred from: a ruthless but effective selection process for the fighting instinct.

In 1835, a new law was passed by Parliament banning all dog fights and recommending severe punishment for offenders. Nevertheless, its practice persisted underground for a long time and is, regretfully, still with us. Any dog-fighting persisting today is as unattractive as it is illegal, and to be condemned by all dog lovers and those whose job it is to uphold the law.

BILLY THE RATKILLER
Other barbaric sports involved different animals, but all were intended to test the bravery of dogs. The game dog was a way to self-realisation and pleasure for the working man. The ancestors of Staffordshire Bull Terriers fought rats

Billy and Rat.
A 19th-century
bronze statuette.

in the pits. Their task was to kill a predetermined number of rats in as short a time as possible and to be faster and more efficient than the other contestants. The famous ratkiller, Billy, killed one hundred rats in five minutes thirty seconds on April 22nd 1823: this was a world record. To do this, Billy had to maintain a rate of one dead rat every three-and-a-half seconds for over five minutes. Anyone who knows about rats will appreciate the danger these creatures pose for a dog. When a rat is cornered it will attack the dog's flews, ears and legs with an extremely painful bite. Small, weak

rodents were not used in these fights, but strong adults. These specimens were readily available, for there was money in it. Many rats could be found around dustbins and sewers in an expanding London and the town authorities engaged rat-catchers to round them up. Only the toughest of them were then used in the pits.

How did Billy manage a rat every three-and-a half seconds? Such a performance was only possible if he could kill them with one bite, breaking their backbones with just one shake before going on to the next. It is not surprising that Billy was greatly used

15

An attack on a donkey. An oil painting c1880.

at stud. Bitches of many different breeds were taken to him: Fox Terriers, Bull Terriers, Staffordshire Bull Terriers and Jack Russell Terriers. A print from 1823 includes Billy's pedigree, which states that his sire was one of the original Bulldogs from a line out of one of the best English Bulldog kennels. Billy's dam was a mixture of Terrier and Bulldog, these being the common ancestors of today's Staffordshire Bull Terriers.

The badger was another victim of these sports. The fighting arena usually accommodated a number of fully-grown badgers on which the dog owners could test their animals' nerve. One technique called 'drawing the badger' involved a long, tunnel-like pipe. At the end of the tunnel, the badger had to wait while the dog crept towards it. The dog had to seize and hold the badger so tightly that the owner could pull both the badger and the dog out. Wagers were staked on how often a dog could pull out a badger in a given time. A badger is a formidable opponent, with an incredibly strong jaw: its skin is extremely thick and difficult for the dog's teeth to penetrate. As a consequence, the dogs' faces would be badly scarred and many a dog would have its jaw broken – a vile and barbaric sport.

In fact, there were few animals that were not set upon by dogs in this manner. Other opponents were apes, wild pigs, horses and donkeys. Reports agree it was very seldom that a dog could be successful when matched against an ape. In the days when such appalling events were commonplace, dogs were allowed to attack tethered donkeys and in no time at all would seize the poor beast by the throat. An oil painting from the middle of the 19th century shows five dogs attacking a donkey. The dog on the right looks very much like today's Staffordshire Bull Terriers. It is interesting to note the indifference of the passing riders.

So much for this "very rude and nasty pleasure" – fighting dogs and animal fights.

SPECIALIST BREEDING
Dogs were bred in the 19th century to fulfil certain purposes: the specialist dog was developed to perform its duty. Bulldogs were used for bull-baiting; Greyhounds to course hares and rabbits; Pointers as gundogs; Retrievers to retrieve game; Collies to herd sheep; and Terriers to catch rats and other vermin. A dog's usefulness was directly related to its success at its allotted task.

Beauty in a dog was no doubt desirable, but the prime consideration was its ability to undertake a specific job. In fact, there were times when aspects of a dog's work were related to quite unpleasing physical appearance: it is often overlooked that not only the temperament of a breed but also its anatomical structure is determined by its designated role. A dog which has to hunt underground for fox must not be long-legged or have a broad chest. Racing dogs require long legs and a deep chest to give heart and lungs plenty of room. The Bulldog was bred with an undershot mouth and a 'laid back' nose, which allowed it to bite its victims easily and effectively and still have room to breathe. Its roached back would have made it easier to approach the bull low to the ground, thus reducing the area of vulnerable flank exposed to the horns.

With the development of the fighting dog breeds, character – gameness, intelligence, endurance and skill – was a prime factor, yet their functional requirements necessitated a suitable body structure. Breeders were quick to realise that, to achieve the best performance from a dog, both character and anatomy must be considered.

THE ENGLISH BULLDOG

The Bulldog could be said to typify certain English characteristics: it takes a lot to ruffle it; it exhibits perseverance, endurance and fierce looks. And if it should come to the worst it will be ready for a fight. "No-one provokes me and remains unpunished!" This has been the English philosophy of life for many a century.

Breed historians have traced the Bulldog back to 1630 from a document concerning the export of two Bulldogs to Spain. From then on, the progress of the breed can be followed through its involvement in bull-baiting. Canine enthusiasts have described the Alaunt as the original ancestor of the large Mastiff-type dogs. Depending on its function, the breed was divided on a size basis. The larger dogs, 'alauntes veutreres', were used for wild boar and stag hunting, and later for bull-baiting, and the smaller dogs were used by butchers as droving

Wasp, Child and Billy. Detail from a hand-coloured engraving, after a painting by H.B. Chalon. London, 15 May 1809.

ABOVE: Bulldogs
and Badger. Detail
from an engraving
from an oil
painting by Malers
Nelion. London,
16 February 1830.

LEFT: Crib and
Rosa. Detail from
a hand-coloured
engraving, after
a painting by
A. Cooper. London,
7 June 1817.

dogs – the 'alaunt of the butcheries'.

By the end of the 19th and the beginning of the 20th century, the original Bulldog was becoming seriously overbred for the show ring. Some ludicrous interpretations of the Breed Standard have resulted in many exaggerations to the form of the breed. In my opinion, these changes have transformed it from a grand and efficient dog into an anatomical cripple. The soundness of the early Bulldog is suggested by the structure of the dogs shown in one famous illustration. These dogs, Wasp, Child and Billy, are the last dogs of a line from the kennels of the famous Duke of Hamilton. By the end of the 18th century, the Duke was one of the foremost breeders of Bulldogs. The footnote on the engraving states that the owner was offered one hundred and twenty guineas for Billy in 1800 – in those times such a sum could buy a house. Around twenty guineas could be expected for one of Billy's puppies: this is certainly more than a worker would bring home for his hard work in a whole year. However, the anatomy of these dogs is much more interesting: straight legs, strong elbows, a muscular, slim body and a head in proportion to the rest. They were very beautiful dogs, those bred by the Duke.

The second piece of evidence is the well-known *Bulldogs and Badger*. This painting was mistakenly attributed to the landscape painter Charles Town but we know today that the artist was Nelion. It dates back to 1816 and a print of it was published in London on February 16th 1830. The conformation of the dogs is short, strong and muscular but they are nevertheless very agile animals. *Crib and Rosa* is a famous engraving by John Scott after a painting by Abraham Cooper which was exhibited in London on June 7th 1817. For over half a century, this remained the most important picture of the Bulldog breed. *Crib and Rosa* was an example to Bulldog enthusiasts and was considered to be their ideal. The soundness and the elegance of the bitch is most impressive: such Bulldogs could move really well – they were healthy, functional dogs.

When we consider the Bulldog ancestors of the Staffordshire Bull Terrier, we imagine specimens like Wasp, Child, Billy and Rosa. They were the Bulldogs of the time of the crossing with Terriers, the Bulldogs which gave the Staffords so many positive attributes, both in terms of temperament and appearance.

THE ENGLISH TERRIER
The second element in the history of the Staffordshire Bull Terrier is the

Terrier, but not the Terrier as we know it today. Sydenham Edwards, a well-known breed enthusiast of the 19th century, described the Terrier in his *Cynographica Britannica* (1800) as "Belligerent, grumpy and irritable but of high intelligence. Always ready for action but without the same obstinacy as the Bulldog, it is extremely fast in attack, which is conducted with skill and special intelligence. The Terrier is unconcerned for its own fate during the attack: its aim is only to cause as much damage as possible. The wild actions of the Terrier protect it and its bite can easily kill its opponent. The Terrier virtually throws itself into the fox hole, drives the fox from hiding and tears it to pieces in its own lair. When matched with a badger, the Terrier can force the slow stubborn victim into the daylight. The Terrier's intelligence is as marked as its courage is great. It can run with Foxhounds, hunt with the Beagle, find the trail for the Greyhound and catch prey with the Spaniel. Wildcats, martens, polecats, ferrets and rats were its alert and ever-ready adversaries. The otter could be driven from the riverbank with the Terrier showing no reluctance for a fray in the wet."

We learn about the anatomy of this Terrier from the Terrier specialist Daniel who wrote in *Field Sports*: "There are two types of Terrier, one is

Terrier. An engraving, after Samuel Howitt. London, 1 September 1808.

Pitch, a Terrier. Engraving, after a painting by Gilpin in 1790. London, 16 November 1810.

Rat hunting. An engraving after a painting by C. Hancock. London, 1 September 1837.

a rough-haired, short-legged dog with a long back, possessing much strength. These dogs were mostly black and tan with white markings. The second type is a smooth-haired dog, mostly reddish brown or black with fawn legs. These dogs have a beautiful shape, much shorter in body and more lively than the first type. Both of these Terrier types are bitter enemies of all hunted animals. When these Terriers are set to fight against badgers, many receive ghastly injuries and yet a well-bred and trained Terrier is often unrivalled and far superior to its opponents."

An engraving of a picture by the renowned English animal painter, Samuel Howitt, was published on September 1st 1808 and shows a rough-haired Terrier with its prey. The strong bone structure of the dog is clear and it certainly appears functionally useful. *Pitch, a Terrier* is an engraving from a painting by Gilpin, dated 1790. It depicts a smooth-haired Terrier type with a wonderful body shape. It is one of the earliest pictures of a Fox Terrier and says much about the first-class anatomy of this dog, the real Terrier type. An engraving from a painting by C. Hancock, published on September 1st 1837, shows four Terriers doing their job as rat-killers. These are small Terrier types, 'all-purpose dogs', that could make themselves useful round the house.

THE STAFFORDSHIRE BULL TERRIER

The Staffordshire Bull Terrier was first recognised as a breed in 1935, but historical records indicate that it is considerably older. The Stafford-type breed developed because of the special requirements demanded of a successful dog-fighter, as opposed to a dog most suited to bull-baiting. As described earlier, the Bulldog would crawl along the ground towards the tethered bull and, at the right moment, seize the bull by its nose and hang on with all its might. Such a technique would not be suitable in the dog-pit, bearing in mind the mentality of the mob, who would not have been entertained by a dog which held back from the fray, so the faster and smarter characteristics of the working Terrier were introduced. After all, the Terrier had time and time again demonstrated its ability to kill its opponent. By crossing a Bulldog with a Terrier, a dog was developed which could provide a tough and varied fight, combining the toughness and stamina of the Bulldog with the speed and intelligence of the Terrier. The quick-witted Terrier was always looking for a chance, correcting a faulty hold and, with singleness of purpose, through repeated attacks on its victims, it would fight until the bitter end.

The 'recipe' for the ideal combination of the two principal breeds was kept top secret in many kennels. The only proof of success was a victorious and bloody encounter in the pit. Depending on the use the dogs were put to, the recipe varied; for the ideal ratter, the Terrier component was dominant. Contemporary authors described a dog as being roughly one-third Bulldog and two-thirds Terrier.

At this point we should consider today's Terrier and today's poor imitation of the original Bulldog. The earlier Bulldog was anatomically perfect and the ideal choice for its designated purpose. The developing 'Bull-and-Terrier' inherited invaluable Bulldog virtues: its character; its unmistakable mixture of courage, singleness of purpose, stamina and bravery; its disregard of pain and readiness for a serious confrontation. The Bulldog temperament was that of a dog whose affection for people was arguably unrivalled in the world of dogs. Because of the Bulldog's special characteristics, it was crossed with many other breeds, probably improving their temperaments considerably: the world of dogs has a lot to thank the Bulldog for! Dogs with Bulldog characteristics are affectionate family dogs – it is hard to believe such good nature goes along with the former practice of bull-baiting, but nevertheless it is true.

The old Bulldog-type working Terrier has, sadly, disappeared from the scene. They were dogs that were biddable and active, and mostly earned their keep as efficient hunters of vermin and good guards of the home.

In the 19th century the Bull-and-Terriers were very useful and if they were successful in the pits they could earn a modest income. Those who describe this as a ruthless selection do so with reason – the breed evolved from a melting pot of cruelty. The resulting dog was a menace to its own kind; its natural instinct was aggression towards other dogs. They fought because of their lust for fighting, not for leadership or for territorial reasons. It follows that today's descendants carry this legacy of former days as well as the positive qualities they have inherited. This fighting instinct, the readiness for a brawl which, in extreme cases, leads to a kill, must be muted by carefully planned breeding and training.

THE BAN ON FIGHTING

The year of 1835 saw the prohibition of all kinds of animal fights, after many attempts by those concerned with animal welfare, and humanitarians in Parliament. It was certainly not an easy victory, for these pursuits had had a great following among all classes for centuries, and the legislation was not very effective against the dog-fighting fraternity. Unlike bear-baiting and bull-baiting, dog-fighting did not require special venues or much organisation. The pits could be made in cellars or back yards, as well as in drinking dens and private houses. Fights were difficult for the police to crack down on, whereas the baiting of larger animals was easier to detect. Dog fights simply went underground and the practice continued. Personal inadequacies and dissatisfaction can lead to antisocial behaviour: owning a successful, death-defying dog may arguably go some way towards relieving such frustrations. Rather like drug-taking today, dog fights could induce a state approaching euphoria.

ORIGINAL TYPE

There are early records of the Bull-and-Terrier which show dogs with a remarkable resemblance to today's Staffords. One of the earliest pictures is George Townley Stubbs's oil painting of 1812. Joseph Dunn, writing in 1950, called it an "outstanding oil painting, a representative portrait of the Bull-and-Terrier at the beginning of the 19th century. It comes closest to today's Staffords." The Stafford expert R.H. Voss commented on this picture in 1946 in *Our Dogs*: "I have never yet seen a Stafford dog quite as good in type and general appearance as this unknown ancestor of the breed, which first saw the light of day at least 135 years ago."

I have an early 19th-century ivory and gold tiepin, which once belonged to the Stafford expert John F. Gordon.

Bull-and-Terrier. Oil painting by George Stubbs, 1812.

Ivory model of a Stafford. Early 19th century, belonging to the collection of John F. Gordon.

ABOVE: *Bull-and-Terrier belonging to Viscount Purst. Oil painting, c1830.*

RIGHT: *Rose, a granddaughter of the dog Billy. Lithograph, after a painting by E. Morley. London, 28 May 1837.*

It is a delicately made, first-class model of a Bull-and-Terrier and it is surprising to see today's head type and anatomy in such an early Bull-and-Terrier – a dog probably anatomically superior to many of today's show Champions.

Another important record of the early Stafford type is an 1830s oil painting of the dogs belonging to Viscount Purst. The well-known dog expert Gerald Massey considered this an important link in the history of the Stafford. I find the parallels between the anatomy of these dogs – the Stubbs dogs and the ivory carving – most interesting. Do not be misled by the rough coats of the Viscount's dogs; coat texture was not important

in those days. These three representations indicate a uniform breed type for the early Bull-and-Terrier and show, at the same time, a striking likeness to the Stafford of today.

A further example is the bitch Rose. A picture of her, from an original engraving after a portrait by E. Morley, published in London on May 28th 1837, was considered by Joseph Dunn to be of such importance that he used it as a cover for his book. The picture is an important historical record, not only because Rose was a good example of how the Bull-and-Terrier looked one hundred years ago, but also because her collar reveals that she had the courage and skill required

ABOVE: First Game. Aquatint, after a painting by Alfred Dedreux, c1840.

RIGHT: Revenge. Aquatint, after a painting by Alfred Dedreux, c1840.

A group of Staffordshire Bull Terriers, in the background a black-and-tan terrier. Oil painting by E. Loderer, 1883.

for bull-baiting. Joseph Dunn continues his description: "Note the small rose ears, the beautiful dark, large round eyes set wide apart, the definite stop, also the excellent 'furrow' extending from nose to the apex of skull and the well-pronounced cheek muscles, the distance from stop to nose and stop to apex of skull, also the squareness and depth of muzzle, with the desired tight lips." He also points out that the white marks on her top lip are not teeth, which is clear on closer examination. Thus Rose, a bitch from the 1830s, exhibits a head similar to one from the 1980s: this continuity in head type for over one hundred and fifty years is a remarkable achievement for a modern breed.

Another interesting feature of this picture is the title, which claims that Rose is the granddaughter of Billy. It

is quite possible that this represents a line of descent from the famous rat-killer of the 1820s, whose record I mentioned earlier. This brings us full circle and supports the relationship between a dog's ability to work and the evolving anatomy of the breed.

Alfred Dedreux was a famous horse artist of his day and, around 1840, he painted his own two dogs, a Greyhound and a white Bull-and-Terrier. We can appreciate his fleet-footed Greyhound but, at the same time, it shows that the "little fat one" can stay with him – speed does not depend just on long legs. The glorious game of these two unlikely companions has been preserved and handed down in an engraving by Jean Pierre Maria Jazet.

The next significant record in the history of the breed is the oil painting

ABOVE: Head study of a Staffordshire Bull Terrier. Terracotta model, c1880.

LEFT: Head study of a Staffordshire Bull Terrier. Oil painting on glass, c1890.

of 1883 by E. Loderer which Gerald Massey describes as a group of Staffordshire Bull Terriers with a black-and-tan Terrier in the background. He states that it has been proven that the dogs were bred solely for fighting purposes and not for show, for dog shows involving the Stafford did not begin until 1935, and he considers it of note that these dogs are depicted with short-cropped ears. There is also in existence a head study of a Staffordshire Bull Terrier which was painted on glass, and analysis revealed that it concealed another picture of a Cocker Spaniel. There is a remarkable similarity between this picture and the E. Loderer dogs. Then there is the terracotta head study, dating from around 1880, which proves the great popularity of the Staffordshire Bull Terrier in England at the end of the 19th century. There were no breeding programmes for dogs, no set standards from a Kennel Club, and no club which maintained a stud book. This breed evolved over more than one hundred years in response to demand for a dog with its particular characteristics and skills.

Joe Mallen (with cap) in the old Cross Guns hotel in Cradley Heath – the headquarters of the Staffordshire Bull Terrier Club.

THE GREAT JOE MALLEN

When a breed and its character have developed over many generations, then the people who once bred the dogs should be carefully studied in order to understand them properly. I have already mentioned Joe Mallen as a pioneer of the modern Stafford breed: in 1972, Joe Mallen celebrated his eighty-second birthday; the *Black Country Bugle* visited the grand old man and talked to him of the past – "the good old days." A look into Joe Mallen's life and memories means going back in time to the birth of the modern Stafford.

Any claim that the new law of 1835 brought about the cessation of dog fights is simply untrue, just as it would be to say that the police have brought the practice under control in the 21st century. The article which follows, written in 1972, proves this to be the

case, and it is not the only evidence: during one of my visits to England, on October 30th 1980, I turned the television to BBC1, where the well-known Stafford expert Ken Bailey reported in an interview that dog fights were still being held in the 1980s. I have seen a photograph which shows Joe Mallen in his heyday: on his left a Stafford and on his right arm a fighting cock. This picture tells of the two great passions of the old man.

Joe Mallen's reminiscences have a place in the breed's history and are relevant to this book, and all Stafford enthusiasts must be grateful to the *Bugle* for capturing such historic detail. They give conclusive evidence of the kind of dogs that went into the melting-pot to form the Stafford. These dogs were the ancestors of the Stafford of today and present-day breeders should expect to detect something of their characteristics in their descendants.

"Joe Mallen is a throwback to a past Black Country era! At eighty-two years of age he is remarkably agile in both mind and body, living proof that 'hard work never killed anybody', for Joe was a 'Big' chainmaker for over fifty years, working in an environment beside which Dante's Inferno pales into a gentle glow. He wielded a hammer, which few men could handle, with a dexterity which made him a legend in a town of tough chainmakers – but it was his dogs, Crossguns Johnson, Gentleman Jim and The Great Bomber, which made his name a household word wherever men talk of Staffordshire Bull Terriers.

"The oldsters will tell you that Joe was a hard man, and his dogs were hard, for in his heyday the Stafford earned his keep or wasn't worth keeping. The pampered pets who perform in today's parade rings may look the part, but as Joe says: 'There's still some good dogs about – but they'n bred the guts out on 'em'."
The Corinthians of the Black Country
"Joe was born in Cradley Heath in 1890, as close to the heart of the Black Country as you can get – a mere eighty-two years ago, but as distant as the Dark Ages from the town today. Like the hamlets which clustered around it, Cradley Heath was a lively centre for the colliers and quarrymen who worked hard and played harder!

"Their status symbol was no shiny car or colour TV, but a dog, whether it be Bull Terrier or Whippet, and a man was usually judged by the canine company he kept. Joe became licensee of *The Cross Guns* in 1921. With Joe's thirst it was just as well! This pub, on the Fiveways at Cradley Heath, became a sporting club for dog men from miles around. Like the Corinthians of the previous century, who embraced blood sports – particularly the prize ring – Joe Mallen's cronies admired, above all else, raw courage whether it be in man or beast. Unlike the Regency dandies, they dressed in moleskin trousers, heavy boots and the proverbial cloth cap with a muffler, or silk scarf if the occasion demanded it, worn flamboyantly over a collarless flannel shirt. It was said that they didn't make collars big enough for chainmakers' necks in those days and the tradition still lingers among the few tough, old characters who survive from that era."

Joe held council in *The Cross Guns*, attracting the wildest and toughest types from around about. This colourful mixture of company drank Joe's ale in an atmosphere that was full of talk about fighting dogs, fighting cocks and rat-killing Terriers. He was happiest in such company. Even in his

Joe Mallen with Stowcote Pride and a fighting cock.

eighties, Joe was a good story-teller, with a never-ending series of anecdotes that transported the listener, and Joe himself, from Joe's comfortable bungalow near Kinver to those old days back at Cradley Heath at the turn of the century. He would tell how, on the eve of his wedding, he had been talking to the village vicar: the vicar had asked young Joe if his father had given him any good hints. Joe replied that his father had told him of three rules in life.

1. Make sure you wear the trousers.
2. Never bet on a slow horse.
3. Make sure your belly button does not get too near your backbone.

"Good tips so far," said the vicar. "Did he say anything else?" "Oh yes," replied Joe. "One thing more he said. 'Do not forget the old proverb, the good die young; so do bad things and live to a ripe old age!'" The vicar was said to have been speechless and did not pursue the subject any further.

The *Black Country Bugle* continues: "The busy canals of Joe's youth have become silted spectres of the great arterial waterways which pumped the blood which kept the Black Country's heart beating! The pit-men are a dead tribe and the hand chainmaker is a very rare species in the scant jungles of the 'Dark Land' today. A great era is dead but its ghosts still haunt the diminishing pit mounds and antiquated pubs which have survived twentieth-century improvements.

"The Act of 1835 placed blood sports outside the bounds of the law, but old customs die hard and Joe Mallen's early days were spent in the company of a cockfighting, hare-coursing, dog-fighting fraternity into whose midst he was born. His father bred Whippets but later turned his interest to Bull Terriers. With such legendary oldsters as Steve Bannister and Jack Garratt, he formulated 'The Rules' which were rigidly adopted whenever matches were made between the fighting dogs of the Black Country. They were remarkably similar to the old prize ring rules, which had governed bare-knuckle fighting a few decades before. They prove that Bull Terrier matches were no mere impromptu, back-street brawls but carefully organised trials of strength, determination and courage fought out under a code of conduct as explicit as it was hard.

"Although Joe held such store in the pedigree of his dogs, he never had the inclination to trace his own origins. It was widely accepted that the Mallens sprang from the loins of the wild, Irish boyos who came across the water to work as navigators when our canals were built at the end of the eighteenth century. The O'Malleys settled in various places along the new waterways and there is little doubt that Joe could trace his ancestry back to this line. He still has the blarney of his Hibernian forebears and an impish sense of humour. The passing generations have hardened the soft Irish burr into the distinctive dialect of the Black Country. In his youth, he was a sudden man with his fists and just as quick to make up a quarrel.

"So much for the melting pot from which the iron in Joe Mallen's character was forged. We find him, in the early years of this century, already a young giant, wielding a hammer with the ease of Thor, and possessed by a raging thirst to purchase a Bull Terrier of his own. He bought his first dog from Jack Challoner, a Salvation Army man who found nothing in the Good Book to prohibit dog fighting.

"Joe was already well versed in the breed, a quick-witted lad with a hunger to learn more. Thus began the apprenticeship in breeding which was to make him the greatest authority in the game in later years. His tutors were his own father, old Steve Bannister and Jack Garratt, men who had spent a lifetime in the game and passed the lore accumulated on to Young Joe.

"He tried his dogs with the best he could find. They didn't merely have to look the part but possess, in full measure, the innate courage and fighting fervour for which the Bull Terrier was renowned. An old saying "As an ounce tew a fighting cock, so a pound tew a dog, an a stoon tew a mon," had governed the blood sports from the first and Joe followed the old tradition – training his dogs to a hair and never over-matching them. He built up a great reputation which even the old men in the game had to admire, gradually producing a strain of fighting dog which had no equal in the land.

"Bull Terrier men came from miles around to put their Champions down with Joe Mallen's breed but, like their canine contestants, usually left Cradley Heath with their tails between their legs and pockets empty."

Joe and the Earl

Another story from the same source relates how one day, after work, Joe had taken a little nap and was woken by his wife with a message that a gentleman in *The Cross Guns* wanted to see him. Joe grumbled at being disturbed but when he was told the visitor had a dog, he hurried to meet the man. Joe was greeted with the words: "I hear, Mr Mallen, that you are something of an authority on the Staffordshire Bull Terrier."

"What I don't know about Staffords isn't worth knowing," was Joe's short and direct reply.

"What do you think of my dog?" the man asked. Joe looked at the animal, which was lying at the feet of the visitor. His first remark was: "How much did you pay for this?"

"£10, in London" was the answer.

"First," said Joe "this is not a Stafford, and second, it is not worth ten pennies, let alone £10!" The gentleman, and the lady with him, were startled by Joe's harsh judgement. "If you want to see what a real Stafford looks like, I'll show you one," said Joe, and he produced his own dog Gentleman Jim. The visitor immediately made Joe an offer for the dog but Joe said he would not part with him for all the tea in China. At this point the visitor introduced himself as the Earl of Dudley. Joe tried, out of respect for the lady, to moderate his harsh words and eventually agreed to sell the Earl a puppy.

After their first meeting, a friendship sprang up between Joe and the Earl. The Earl owned all the mining rights to the land on which Joe lived, but nevertheless, in his own sport, the landlord of *The Cross Guns* was as revered as the King of England. Joe was invited to Himley Hall a few months after selling the puppy to the Earl to give an opinion on the puppy. At the entrance, the head gamekeeper pleaded with Joe not to buy the puppy back as it was the best dog he had ever seen at retrieving from the water. Joe was not going to be influenced by such appeals and was determined to give an objective opinion of the dog. When he saw it, he remarked that its back was long so not quite correct, but otherwise he found it a good specimen and said he was quite willing to buy it back. The Earl appreciated Joe's honesty but, to the delight of his gamekeeper, did not want to sell the dog.

GENTLEMAN JIM

From the *Black Country Bugle* come further tales of famous Staffords:

"The tale of how Joe came to own Gentleman Jim – the prize Stafford of them all – is a story in itself. Jack Dunn, from Quarry Bank, was a workmate of Joe's at Griffins. Joe had given him a bitch called Triton Judy who produced a litter, sired by Brindle Mick, the founder of the 'M' line. To cut a long story short, the future Champion was 'left in the nest' and Joe bought him from Jack Dunn for £1. He named his new pup Gentleman Jim and it was the start of a wonderful partnership.

"Joe took Gentleman Jim to Crufts in 1938 and got two seconds in the puppy class. Despite his obvious potential in the show ring, Gentleman Jim was no pampered show dog. He had to earn his keep and reputation in the time-honoured manner, fighting and defeating any challenger who turned up at *The Cross Guns*. Joe recalls that he fought and defeated three game dogs in one afternoon and lost a fang in the process. All this went on in the months leading up to the 1939 Crufts show. In that period, Gentleman Jim proved he was not only cast in the mould of physical perfection, but possessed the tremendous courage and gameness which was a famous attribute in the Mallen strain.

"The year 1939 was Gentleman Jim's year! For the first time the breed was granted Challenge Certificates and Gentleman Jim became the first ever Staffordshire Bull Terrier Supreme Champion. Joe Mallen's pride in the success was shared by his Black Country compatriots. Men came from all over the country to see the great dog. As Joe puts it: "We never closed. If we turned 'em out at closin' time, the policeman on'y brought 'em back agen'."

"Gentleman Jim's services were in great demand and he produced several Champions, passing on the superb

Ch. Gentleman Jim, the first dog Champion of the breed, 1939.

qualities of the Mallen line and earning Joe a lot of money. The Second World War stopped Gentleman Jim from winning further and he died in 1947, the year that the Championships were resumed, but his progeny listed below kept the title in the family.

1947 Widneyland Kim
1948 Fearless Red of Bandits
1949 Jim's Double of Wychbury
1949 Eastbury Lass

"Joe has a thousand anecdotes about the old days, like when his pal Harry Pegg, who owned Fearless Joe, a noted fighter, received a challenge from Mr Croom, the well-known Gloucester fancier, to take his dog down to do battle with the Croom Champion. Joe Mallen went along and in his own words: "Harry's dog won in a very short time – tuther wouldn't have it." With the contest so curtailed, Mr Croom invited Joe and Harry to a badger dig in some woodland on his estate."

THE DEATH OF FEARLESS JOE

"Although the Corinthian sporting bucks of the previous century had enjoyed the sport with a small breed of Staffords, Mr Croom preferred Jack Russells in his pursuit of Brock. Joe describes how they found the badger earth and Mr Croom sent one of his Terriers into it. The dog reappeared in a short time, bitten through the leg and limping heavily. "Brocks at home," shouted Mr Croom, putting his second Jack Russell into the earth. However, he returned from the hole bleeding heavily from the nose and jaws. By this time Fearless Joe, who Harry Pegg held on a leash, was getting excited and pulled out of his collar and plunged into the burrow.

"That's done it, Harry," said Joe. "If he tecks ote we shall have tew dig 'em booth out." That is exactly what they did. After digging three or four yards they saw the earth moving. Joe probed around with the Badger tongs, got a grip and hauled the badger out.

"Fearless Joe's jaws were fastened on the badger's throat but he rolled off as he was dragged to daylight and lay, savagely injured, on the bloodstained earth. They carried him to the pump and sluiced water over him. This cleansing operation revealed the extent of his injuries. One eye had been scraped from its socket, his snout and lips were torn to shreds and the forepart of his body was like a piece of raw liver. Mr Croom wanted to shoot Fearless Joe on the spot but Harry Pegg would not hear of it. He and Joe arrived back at *The Cross Guns* at 3 am with the dog still barely alive – but he did not last until dawn! Joe had also brought the badger back with him and kept it in the cellar of *The Cross Guns* until it died. Like Joe says: "Ther's no dog born as would stond a chance with a badger in his own earth."

"We reckon that few men ever stood a chance of beating Joe at anything he set his mind to. Nowadays you can find him in his local at Kinver, usually playing dominoes. They reckon he never loses at that game either and that he sometimes cheats a little – but that's only the Irish coming out in him. He still does a good day's work on his son-in-law's farm and lives in a comfortable bungalow at White Hill, surrounded by the trophies and accoutrements of a past era. The years have been kind to this craggy, old Black Countryman who reigned like a king from his palace at the old *Cross Guns* during the most turbulent and memorable decades that Cradley Heath knew. Like the dogs he bred, Joe keeps a grip on life which doesn't seem likely to slacken for at least twenty years."

2 DEVELOPMENT OF THE BREED

The American, Steve Eltinge, sees the position of Staffords in English society in the industrial revolution as something of a class symbol: coalminers, foundry workers and blacksmiths chose the Bull-and-Terrier as a companion – a dog they could identify with. But he finds such dogs less popular among the middle classes, who tended to be apprehensive of their reputation.

The name Stafford only really came into use in the 1920s. It arose from their place of origin – Staffordshire, the heart of the Black Country. Initially these dogs were identified by various names: Bull-and-Terrier, Pit Dog or Fighting Terrier. Joseph Dunn, one of the pioneers of the breed, writing of the years 1910 to 1934, describes ten families who had owned such dogs for generations; though there were no real pedigrees, all the dogs were similar in appearance.

Joseph Dunn, the founder of the Staffordshire Bull Terrier Club, in 1935.

The suggestion that the Staffordshire Bull Terrier should be recognised by the Kennel Club met with much opposition from the fanatical followers of the breed. Their concern was that this would automatically transform the Stafford into one of the beauty breeds, and that competitions for show prizes and titles of Champion would mean an end to the special characteristics of the breed. John F. Gordon reported that at one of the first shows an argument developed as 'old-timers' grumbled at the ringside: one fanatic shouted "If a Stafford hasn't got it in his heart, then he's not a real Stafford. That's what they mean to do – they want a Stafford without the real old heart!"

Nevertheless, those who wanted to see the breed progress persevered in their efforts to attain recognition for the Stafford and its inclusion in the British show world. They were sure they could retain the temperament inherited through many generations and at the same time achieve a uniformity of breed anatomy and type – and they were right.

THE STAFFORDSHIRE BULL TERRIER CLUB

It was thanks to Joseph Dunn that the breed attained Kennel Club recognition on May 25th 1935. To celebrate, Dunn invited his friends to a Stafford fanciers meeting. Among them was his friend Joe Mallen who was, as I have said, the landlord of *The Cross Guns* at Cradley Heath, South Staffordshire, who had been breeding Staffords for over forty years. About forty to fifty breeders met at *The Cross Guns* and founded the Original Staffordshire Bull Terrier Club. Among the founder members was a Garret, whose family was known to have bred Staffords for many generations, extending back over

eighty years into the middle of the 19th century. The club's founder members elected a committee of eight well-known breeders, each of whom had been active in the breed for over twenty years. The first president, elected at this meeting, was Jack Barnard, the owner of Paddock Kennels. At the same meeting, the first Breed Standard, which had been worked out by Joseph Dunn and some other old breeders, was dispensed with, for reasons which will be revealed later on in this book.

The Kennel Club accepted the formation of the new club but its proposed name was rejected: the Bull Terrier Club, a long-standing member of the Kennel Club, had objected to the use of the word 'Original', but agreed to Staffordshire Bull Terrier Club. After Staffords had been accepted by the Kennel Club, they made their first appearance at the Great Hertfordshire Open Show, held on June 20th 1935 in Hatfield. There were two Stafford classes and twenty-seven dogs entered. There is a photograph in existence from this show which gives an idea of the type of dog exhibited. The newly formed club arranged its first speciality show at Cradley Heath on August 17th 1935. Sixty dogs were presented to the judge, evidence enough that by then the old-timers were supporting the

ABOVE: The Great Hertfordshire Open Show, held in Hatfield on 20 June 1935.

new club. The early pioneers included a number of names which crop up frequently in the history of the Stafford. First is Joseph Dunn; the club is indebted to him for its foundation and for the recognition of the breed by the Kennel Club. He was secretary of the Staffordshire Bull Terrier Club for many years and kept everything going. Joe Mallen kept his own kennels for forty years and his dogs were always in peak condition. His top dog was Ch. Gentleman Jim, who became a milestone in the history of the breed and is behind nearly every Stafford today. Gerald Dudley

exhibited first-class dogs in top condition for nearly thirty-five years: at one time he had seven Champions in his own kennel. His hallmark was that all his Staffords displayed not simply the correct anatomy but also the true temperament of the breed.

Among the pioneers of the breed was John F. Gordon, and his kennel, Bandits, was one of the best in the country. Jack Barnard noted that every animal in his kennel was always in top condition, sound, of correct breed type and possessing the real Stafford temperament. John F. Gordon, through his books, did much to awaken interest and understanding in the breed, and his love for the Stafford comes across readily. Jack Barnard, the first president of the new club, wrote the first book about the breed, in 1935. His dog, Jim the Dandy, was such a typical example that he was kept in mind by breeders during the preparation of the first Standard.

All these men devoted their energy, time and expertise to achieving the recognition that the Staffordshire Bull Terrier deserved. They had many friends and helpers, whom it would be impossible to name, and these idealists soon gained the satisfaction of knowing that their work bore fruit.

CHAMPIONSHIP STATUS

In order to achieve so-called Championship status from the Kennel Club, the new club needed to register 750 pure-bred Staffords. When the combined yearly registrations reached that figure, Challenge Certificates (CCs) became available at Championship shows. The club achieved this in 1938, in just three years, and at the National Championship Show in Birmingham, on November 8th and 9th 1938, the Kennel Club offered the first CCs for Staffords. The road to top honours was finally open.

The first two breed Champions were awarded their titles at Bath on May

Ch. Lady Eve. The first bitch Champion in the breed, 1939.

4th 1939. Both animals had three CCs from different judges. One has already been mentioned, Ch. Gentleman Jim, and the other was the bitch Ch. Lady Eve. Interestingly, these first Champions were both patched whites.

H.N. Beilby, writing in 1943, stated that the success of the club from 1935 to 1942 was owed primarily to its secretary and founder Joe Dunn. It was no doubt useful that a relatively large number of members lived in close proximity; this helped to promote close co-operation between many breeders and an active show-going fraternity. By 1937, many Stafford fanciers had begun meeting around London, and this resulted in the formation of the Southern Counties Staffordshire Bull Terrier

Club. The first president was the popular film actor Tom Walls, of whom more later.

The Southern Counties Staffordshire Bull Terrier Club was extremely successful and stimulated many new initiatives. Today, the breed has 18 regional clubs, and these cover the whole of the country. They do not compete against one another, but work together for the good of the breed.

Staffordshire Bull Terrier breed clubs, in alphabetical order, are

Alyn and Deeside Staffordshire Bull Terrier Club
Downlands Staffordshire Bull Terrier Club
East Anglian Staffordshire Bull Terrier Club
East Midland Staffordshire Bull Terrier Club
Merseyside Staffordshire Bull Terrier Club
Morecombe Bay and Cumbria Staffordshire Bull Terrier Club
Northern Counties Staffordshire Bull Terrier Club (since 1943)
North Eastern Staffordshire Bull Terrier Club
Northern Ireland Staffordshire Bull Terrier Club
North of Scotland Staffordshire Bull Terrier Club
North West Staffordshire Bull Terrier Club (since 1946)
Notts and Derby Staffordshire Bull Terrier Club
Potteries Staffordshire Bull Terrier Club
Scottish Staffordshire Bull Terrier Club
Southern Counties Staffordshire Bull Terrier Club (since 1937)
Staffordshire Bull Terrier Club
Staffordshire Bull Terrier Club of South Wales
Western Staffordshire Bull Terrier Society

In Ireland, the Staffordshire Bull Terrier fanciers
are served by two clubs:
Irish Staffordshire Bull Terrier Association
Irish Staffordshire Fanciers Club

There are several other countries which have specialist clubs which cater for the breed: Australia, Germany, Eire, Finland, Holland, Canada, New Zealand, South Africa, Zimbabwe and two clubs in the USA. The Staffordshire Bull Terrier is making its way in the world.

JUDGING AND BREEDING MATERIAL

Joe Mallen's memories, with which the historical section of the book closed, are an excellent illustration of the identification of the Stafford with the people of the Black Country. In 1981 we visited the Potteries Staffordshire Bull Terrier Club show held at Stoke-on-Trent. There were 200 Staffords at this one show – an incredible number by German standards. We met and talked to several breeders and got to know the people and dogs: L. Hemstock, Eddie and Mary Pringle, Fred Phillips, Bill Hodkingson, L.J. Pearce, and the judges G. Dudley and A. Harkness. They were all very willing to give us an insight into the breeding stock and the priorities set by the breeders and judges. Over the years we have made more journeys to see Staffords in England, and in 1982 we once again visited the Potteries. On this occasion there were 262 Staffords, and again there was animated discussion of the judging and breeding material.

The 18 regional clubs are well-supported and hold yearly shows; these are always well-attended, and include a large number of foreign visitors. Of equal importance are the 38 Championship shows in the year, with anything up to 300 Staffords at each one, and there are also many smaller shows. One could show a Stafford almost every week at a show licensed by the Kennel Club. The enthusiasm for these shows is remarkable: the former pit-dog has conquered the show ring and features in large numbers at the bigger shows – evidence of its popularity in Britain.

Apart from our yearly visit to Crufts, where 300 Staffords usually compete for the big win, we have gone to three large club shows. The largest was the Golden Jubilee show in 1985, with a record number of over 400 dogs, twenty-six Champions among them. The impression I got here was that, at least recently, there have been only a few carefully built bloodlines, and a few kennels each adhering to its distinctive breed type. The majority of breeders only keep between one and three dogs for breeding and simply breed, and show, their dogs for enjoyment and pleasure, relying mostly on their experience, intuition and breeder's luck. The British and overseas visitors discussed breeding techniques with the committee from the Potteries, who answered many of our questions. I argued against unplanned breeding techniques and said that in my opinion the breeding of Staffords in England was like the weekly bingo game: their breeding was a game of chance, not skill.

The corollary is that a breed with so many hundreds of dedicated breeders has a very large and widespread gene pool. This will inevitably result in a non-uniform anatomy throughout the breed, although it reduces some of the dangers associated with in-breeding. If health, ability and intelligence are given priority over beauty, then such a wide gene pool is advantageous, though it does not result in many large dominant kennels, or in dominant male bloodlines in any geographical area. Many enthusiastic Stafford breeders work hard to breed good dogs and all have a chance of success in breeding a show winner.

Under such circumstances it is remarkable, an outstanding achievement, that a single stud dog can produce fourteen Champions. Such a dog was Ch. Black Tusker. In his show career he gained fourteen CCs and eight reserve CCs. This is a formidable achievement considering the large number of dogs competing at Championship shows – marvellous, and, as I have implied, an exception.

Of other beautiful animals which I have seen and admired, I begin with the most successful Stafford in 1985, Ch. Belnite Blitzkrieg. This dog was Best of Breed at Crufts in 1985 against over 150 Staffords; he was also Best In Show at the Golden Jubilee show, out of over 400 Staffords, twenty-six of which were Champions.

ABOVE: Ch. Black Tusker. Top English dog in 1978, with 14 CCs, 8 RES CCs. One of the foremost stud dogs with 14 English Champion offspring.

BELOW: Ch. Belnite Blitzkrieg. Best of Breed, Crufts 1985, and Best In Show, Golden Jubilee Show 1985.

*Belnite Black
Warrior.
Grandfather
of Ch. Belnite
Blitzkrieg and
Int. Ch. Belnite
Dark Narcissus.*

*Ch. Belnite
Belladonna.*

*Ch. Rendorn Apollyon.
Born 11 November 1985,
CC at Crufts 1987.*

*Ch. Rendorn
Delta Dawn.*

At this show the regional Staffordshire Bull Terrier clubs celebrated fifty years since the recognition of the breed.

Blitzkrieg was bred by Billy McKnight in his small kennel in Ireland. I visited the Belnite kennel in Belfast and was impressed with the uniformity of the breed type and the clarity of the owner's conception of the breed. This can be seen from pictures of Belnite Black Warrior, the grandfather of Blitzkrieg and Ch. Belnite Belladonna. McKnight is only one of many enthusiastic breeders, and there are many breeders in Britain who produce beautiful and very good-tempered Staffords. This book would burst at the seams if I were to include all the important Staffords.

A successful kennel is based on a top-class bitch. With this in mind, I have chosen to end this section with two exceptionally lovely bitches: Ch. Rendorn Apollyon, who was Crufts Best Bitch 1987 and Ch. Rendorn Delta Dawn.

REGISTRATIONS

The popularity of the breed is reflected in the number of Staffords registered with the Kennel Club each year. There is no obligation for breeders to register their puppies, so a considerable proportion of British dog breeding simply involves the breeder providing a handwritten pedigree, where the breeder's signature signifies that the dog is pure-bred, and that is all. The British pet market, which only wants family pets, is quite happy with such pedigrees. Only those who want to show their dogs or breed from them need to have them registered with the Kennel Club, thus the true number of Staffords bred in Britain cannot be taken from these registrations alone. It is estimated that this figure only represents two-thirds of the actual number of dogs bred.

Since 1982, the Stafford has become the most popular Terrier breed, taking the place of the West Highland White. And the Stafford was ninth most popular of all breeds in 1987, a performance breeders can be proud of.

THE DANGERS OF POPULARITY

Popularity can present dangers for a breed. I know fine breeds that have suffered both in temperament and anatomy due to the 'also-breeders', a term I use for those who breed for what I consider the wrong reasons. Consequently, such breeds have lost a lot of popularity. After the second world war, particularly between 1946 and 1949, the popularity of the Stafford experienced a boom. It was the heyday of 'wild breeding' without Kennel Club registration, so figures for these years merely reflect the trend.

Bill Hodgkinson with Betchgreen Dandy.

These 'mushroom' breeders, who bred dogs in cellars like mushrooms, and whose sole aim was to earn quick and easy money, were deplored by experts. The figures from the 1950s reflect a decrease in mushroom breeders, because it became less easy to make money with Staffords, especially as there was little overseas interest at that time. As a result, prices remained at a sensible level.

The registration figures from the 1980s are arresting: there seemed to be a steady demand for puppies, without the prices climbing sky-high. Such popularity justifies the extent of today's breeding. It is to be hoped that in future years the Stafford will achieve the goodwill of all dog lovers and it will be thanks to the advantages that this all-purpose dog possesses.

To round off this section, we shall return to the people who breed, love and care for Staffords. On one of my visits I met Bill Hodgkinson, the breeder of the wonderful Betchgreen Staffords. One look at his mighty Betchgreen Dandy showed how the large-framed Staffords of the older type were kept in good condition in the 1980s. Bill also showed us his fighting cocks, the breeding of which were his second hobby. A gamecock would rest calmly in Bill's arms, but turn into a fierce fire-devil in seconds. Joe Mallen and his friends are not with us today but the old interest lingers. In Northern Ireland we had a highly interesting evening at a local haunt of Stafford fanciers. There was a lot of activity in this old pub! Listening to tales for a whole evening, drinking Guinness from the barrel, it is plain how much the Stafford means to these people and will doubtless continue to do so.

GERMANY

Members of the British Army stationed in Germany were responsible for the first Staffordshire Bull Terrier litters born there. Many British families stationed in Germany brought

Red Marquita of Bandits (Tara). Born 26 February 1971. The imported foundation bitch of the kennel vom Pirat, pictured with Hans Lachat.

Eddie Pringle with Red Rose vom Pirat.

their four-legged members of the family with them. On April 12th 1969 the first litter of Staffords was born in Germany. This litter founded the kennel Towstaff, belonging to Mr and Mrs Townsend in Viersen. The four males and three females were the first to be registered in Germany. The second litter was registered in 1975 and was bred by Major Garbutts from Minden. I remember this litter well, as I was the breed warden who checked the puppies. These litters belonging to

British families were completely integrated into their domestic life.

Hans and Edith Lachat, from Heidelberg, were the first German breeders. They registered their kennel vom Pirat in 1973, and on February 7th 1974 their first litter was born. I saw the little bitch puppy Aisa. Hans and Edith Lachat were the Staffordshire Bull Terrier pioneers in Germany, and speedily overcame any teething problems. The Lachat foundation bitch was Red Marquita of

LEFT: Bitch import Rufhill
Gaiety Girl.

BELOW LEFT: Imports: Int.
Ch. Ramlyn Copper Glow and
Int. Ch. Rufhill Gaiety Girl.

BELOW: Import Int.
Ch. Threapwood Nobleman
of Betchgreen.

Bandits. Her pet name was Tara and she was born on February 26th 1971; she travelled to many shows with the Lachats to advertise the breed. The lovely bitch Red Rose vom Pirat was bred by the Lachats; she came from their eighteenth litter and was one of the last from this pioneer kennel. Hans and Edith Lachat died before they could reap the rewards they deserved for all their hard work.

It was through this kennel that a number of Staffords came to Germany, including Rufhill Gaiety Girl, Ramlyn Copper Glow and Threapwood Nobleman of Betchgreen. It took several exploratory journeys to Britain before these dogs reached Germany: it was not easy to buy good breeding stock for export.

Although this pioneer work was undertaken with great enthusiasm, no planned breeding programme was evolved and there was no careful building of German bloodlines, so that the descendants of the imported dogs did not show a uniform breed type. It is important not to be misled by the many titles the imported dogs have won. Germany has too many national, international and world Champions; Hans Lachat declared once that it would be possible to take a goat on a lead into the ring at a European show and win a Champion title and his remark is a fair comment on the lack

of qualifications and experience of many of the judges, who have no idea how to cope with a new breed.

In the footsteps of Hans Lachat came the Flambeau kennels of Hans Fackel in Kretsch (founded in 1977). Ingo Pruss has been, together with Hans Lachat, one of the most active breeders. The first litter from his kennel was born on November 10th 1977. Since then there have been a number of litters and many of his dogs have won prizes. Other active promoters of the breed include Frau Grietje Feiken-Preuss who founded the Devilmoors kennel in 1976; Inge Eisenmann (Moguntia); Werner Weinert (vom Husarendenkmal); Rainer Flemming (Rainbow); Georg Scherzer (von der Alter Veste); and in recent years, Chris and Leslie Porter (Cartier). All the breeders had a difficult time establishing the Bull Terrier in Germany between 1960 and 1980, for the interests of the Stafford fanciers were administered by the Bull Terrier Club and as the 'odd ones out' they had little say in the running of the club and got little help from it.

There are a number of very good dogs in Germany but it has been a handicap that the imported dogs really did not complement the existing stock in Germany. Only now are a few kennels starting to create a kennel type.

In 1988, the First International Bull Terrier Club 1988 (ISBC '88) e. V. was founded. It promotes the Staffordshire Bull Terrier on the continent, while at the same time running a beneficial breeding programme. It needs much more work to popularise the Stafford in Germany, particularly in light of the Dangerous Dogs' legislation that is being considered at the time of going to press.

The new laws, proposed after a six-year-old was killed in Hamburg by a Pit Bull, will affect many breeds of dog, including the Stafford.

At the time of writing, measures are being considered to ban the keeping of certain breeds, mandatory wearing of leash and muzzle in public places, the prohibition to breed, import and trade certain breeds, and even the confiscation and killing of dogs.

The Stafford is proposed as one of the most dangerous of breeds – even though there have been no incidents of a Stafford biting anyone. Needless to say, the effect of such measures will be disastrous for the breed and its enthusiasts.

AMERICA
It has not been easy for the Stafford to find recognition or admirers in the USA, largely because the Staffords exported at the turn of the century were initially crossed with other breeds, resulting in the Pit Bull Terrier and the American Staffordshire Bull Terrier. Both these breeds originated in America and have many admirers, though the Pit Bull Terriers are still not recognised as a breed, except as a mixture of breeds designed for dog-fighting. The selection of breeding stock is, as in the Middle Ages, based on the success of the fighter, and the authorities have so far been unable to control fighting. All kinds of 'fighters' have been crossed, regardless of their breed, which has resulted in a wide variety of dog described as Pit Bull Terriers, making it impossible to give a general description, as can be done with pedigree dogs.

The American Staffordshire Bull Terrier was recognised by the American Kennel Club in 1936. The main difference between the American and English Staffords is that the American cousins are substantially larger and longer in the leg, resulting in an anatomy with different proportions; the head shape is also different.

The Staffordshire Bull Terrier only received official recognition in the USA in 1974. Since then it has found many friends in the US and its progress has been well documented in *The Staffordshire Bull Terrier in America*. The enthusiasm with which the Stafford has been introduced to shows and Obedience trials in the United

States is impressive. As might be expected, the breed there is based on good imports from England. Stafford fanciers in America say that Staffordshire Bull Terriers have until recently not been particularly popular. All the same, the breed has slowly found followers, thanks to enthusiasts, and it is on these few dozen devoted Stafford lovers that the future of the breed in America will depend. As in Germany, the breed could become very popular, but it will take a great deal of enthusiasm and effort by breeders.

EUROPE

The Stafford has been popular for some considerable time in Holland where there are a number of breeders with one or two Staffords who have worked towards quality breeding. In 1970 I judged the Dutch Bull Terrier Club Show where about fifty Staffords were presented to me. The winner at this show was a handsome black and white dog. I feel that the owners' interpretation of the Stafford and its breeding was similar to the views of Stafford breeders in England; they

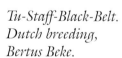

*Tu-Staff-Black-Belt.
Dutch breeding,
Bertus Beke.*

*Nine-year-old
import in Sweden.*

particularly loved their dog's superb character, its real Stafford temperament.

In 1988 I visited Sweden to look at the breed there. As in Holland, the desire to breed a 'working' terrier is widespread. Sweden began registering Staffords in the 1970s, and until recently had few enthusiasts. There are still only a few pioneers working for the breed, but once someone has owned a Stafford they are converted, and promote the breed wherever they can.

Austria and Switzerland show a very similar picture, with the breed at a very early stage: there are one or two enthusiasts who care for the breed and try to promote it, but with little encouragement from other dog lovers. Both countries have the potential to develop the breed.

With the exception of Holland, Sweden and Germany, active breeding of the Stafford on the continent is still at the development stage. It represents a challenge for the First International Stafford Bull Terrier Club.

3 CHARACTER OF THE STAFFORD

It is not easy to describe the main characteristics of a dog in a few words. Dog lovers will define their canine companions in different ways, all having their own opinions. The character of the Staffordshire Bull Terrier must best be described by one who has made them his life's companion and is happy with the breed. If the reader finds he can subsequently say: "Yes, this is how I imagined this type of dog, and this is how it has been!", then I will have brought together two beings meant for each other.

DOGS AND THEIR OWNERS

Way back in 1938, the English author Michael Chance visited many well-known personalities owning dogs in England, and made a surprising discovery: "I originally chose the dog owners I visited because of their position and reputation but I came to the conclusion that a certain kind of person was attracted to a certain kind of dog. I think it is true that the dog mirrors the character of his master and this gives us considerable room for thought."

In writing about Buller, Bella and all Tom Walls's other companions I, too, suggest that the man and the animals grow to resemble each other during their lives, so let us now follow Michael Chance on his visit to Tom Walls, a well-known actor of the time.

"It is Mr Tom Walls's good fortune – and that of his friends as well – that he is blessed with the gift of enthusiasm. Whether he is training horses, breeding dogs or other animals, acting for films or the stage, he brings to bear upon the occupation of the moment a youthful and infectious zest that might well be the envy of many a man far younger than himself.

"Few people need to be reminded that in 1932 he owned and trained the Derby winner in April the Fifth, or

Buller and Co. – flying dogs.

Photo: Stanley M Ballance.

that subsequently his son, Tom Walls Jnr, won the Grand Military race on another home-trained animal. But it is not generally known that the real Tom Walls is a farmer – of unusual type. For on a small scale, but along model lines, he is a practical farmer with a genuine affection for each individual animal. His prize-winning ducks and his Champion drake cluster round his feet with genuine confidence. The black-faced sheep and their lambs, grazing in the field where a fine jumper has been schooled, press so closely at his heels that he cannot bear to think of them in relation to mint sauce. His Jersey cows hurry fearlessly to him at his call. His fine cockerels walk serenely around, scorning the noisy flutter of lesser birds. Jack, the prize boar, responds with most unusual and unpig-like sprightliness at the first sound of his master's voice. In a word, although he has trained himself to be a first-class actor, and has worked hard to become a successful racehorse owner, Mr Walls is a natural animal lover.

"To see Mr Walls standing on the lawn of his Ewell house, hemmed in by a leaping, highly excited crowd of eight or ten Staffordshire Bull Terriers; to see Mrs Walls's Pekingese miraculously maintaining his Oriental detachment somewhere in the midst of

Tom Walls with Buller.

Photo: Stanley M. Ballance.

this hurly-burly; to notice two or three cats lazily and aloofly watching the proceedings from a few yards' range, and to watch dogs and cats feeding together, is to know that Mr Walls not only loves all animals, but possesses the power of giving them something more than a negative kind of happiness.

"It is, however, plain for all to see that his chief favourites are his dogs, his Staffordshire Bull Terriers. For twenty-five years he has owned and bred this breed, first the white dogs, then the brindle variety, and now, for the last eleven years, the old but recently revived Staffordshire pit-dog.

As an exhibitor in the show ring he has achieved considerable successes, although he is unshakeable in his determination that no dog shall be shown in the ring whose sporting qualities have not been abundantly tested beforehand.

THE DOG BULLER
"Undisputed and indisputable king of all his dogs is Buller, a lovable courageous old fellow with jaws of steel and muscles of iron. Buller is one of the most attractive dogs I know, combining as he does the 'sloppiness' of the Bull Terrier with an almost terrifying controlled vitality that can

only be compared with Jack Dempsey at his best. Gentle in repose, a whirlwind in action, Buller has to be seen to be believed; while the loud crack of his jaws, on the rare occasions that he misses an awkwardly bouncing ball, is well-nigh incredible even when it is heard. Not one of all the dogs whose memories remain fresh in Mr Walls's mind, not even Mouldy Jacques, ever established himself so firmly in his master's affections as has Buller. Bred by Mr Walls himself, Buller sleeps in his master's room, and accompanies him everywhere where dogs are allowed and to many places where they are not. And Tom Walls grows daily more emphatic that he has never owned and never will own a dog so rich in courage, strength, intelligence, obstinacy, and general lovableness as Buller. I, if I may do so, agree with him. Buller is a dog in ten thousand.

BELLA THE BITCH
"Of the many stirring tales Mr Walls has to tell concerning his dogs, past and present, none is more delightful than the story of Bella, the bitch with so strong a mothering complex that in certain moods she is wholly unable to resist the temptation to adopt some young creature. Baby chickens are as safe and warm with her as with their own mother, and should another bitch be whelping, Bella will sit solicitously outside the door.

"It once happened that a cat and her newly arrived family were installed in a barn not a hundred yards from Bella's quarters, and Bella immediately became kitten-minded. Choosing the moment of the mother cat's temporary absence, Bella one day tiptoed to the barn, and seizing a kitten gently in her mouth bore it off to her kennel; then, hurrying back to the barn, she kidnapped another. At this point the mother cat returned and, missing her two kittens and sensing what had occurred, hastened to Bella's kennel and recovered one of her children. It was then that Mr Walls, glancing by chance out of the window, saw Bella and the mother cat, each carrying a kitten in her mouth, *passing each other in the drive* as they made haste to their respective homes!

"There is no doubt about it – Mr Walls is not only devoted to his dogs, but shares a vast amount of fun with them."

THE ALL-PURPOSE DOG
Mary Pringle is quite justified in her disappointment at the Kennel Club's revised Standard. It omits the words 'foremost all-purpose dog'. This may not have seemed an important phrase to those who revised the Standard, but for Stafford fanciers its omission is

grave. Before taking a dog into one's home the deciding factor is: "Is this dog suitable for my family and myself; will it suit our lifestyle and our environment?" There are only a few anatomical features which will make a dog unsuitable. What is of greater importance is the dog's temperament, its ability to adapt, its good nature, its love of exercise and its sociability towards people, other animals and its surroundings.

It is exactly such a dog that the Stafford breeder works towards. The fighting dog, the gladiator from the pit, was left behind long ago; such dogs belonged to another age. Since the new start of the breed in the thirties, the objective has been the friendly family dog, the children's friend, the dog for the average man.

THE ONE-MAN DOG
There is a saying "Hail fellow, well met!". When applied to a dog it means that when it is greeted by a stranger it shows its pleasure and immediately strikes up a friendship. As I have said before, many, too many, dog owners misunderstand the nature of such dogs. Even the internationally well-known dog psychologist Konrad Lorenz was very hard on them; he described them as *kalfaktor*, 'fawning'. Lorenz compared them to jackal-like breeds and rejected

them with contempt, describing them as the antithesis of the glorious 'one-man dogs', noble wolf-blooded animals.

He feels this way because of something deep-rooted in man's subconscious. Just as man sees himself subject only to a supernatural power, call it God or what you will, so he sees creatures on earth as subject to his own will: thus his dog must only acknowledge him. This kind of one-man dog is the creation of a man who is proud, jealous and has a complete misunderstanding of the dog's social conduct; such a man will readily reject a dog which he considers fawning.

THE SOCIABLE DOG
From our look at history we know that the fighting dog had to get on with people; they needed an incredible amount of self-assurance, self-reliance, hard-headedness, and keenness to be able to stand on their own and withstand the many trials of the pit. Just such friendliness towards people, together with self-assurance, prompts a dog to appreciate a welcome distraction in a stranger, and enjoy a new friendship. "Hello, nice to meet you!" This is really what the fighting dog feels when it meets strangers. When the new-found human friend returns this friendship and makes a fuss of the dog, he should

The Stafford is an open and friendly character.

A well-trained Stafford is entirely trustworthy with children.

not consider its approach to be just flattery. People who dislike fawning dogs do not take the trouble to consider what the dog is saying: they have already passed sentence on its nature. A friendly dog, in the 21st century, is a pleasure to own. An unfriendly dog results in a lot of problems, but few people realise this. There are too many dogs which are nervous, which growl or change into hysterical and aggressive creatures towards anything new which might threaten. This is not self-assurance, but fear.

A dog with a good temperament is intelligent and fearless. It will greet a stranger with positive expectations and will take pleasure from the offer of friendship; it has no reason to feel that in doing so it betrays its owner. Anyone who does not like such open, friendly and happy self-assurance in a dog should buy another more complicated breed, not a Stafford.

STAFFORDS AND CHILDREN

It is due to the disposition of the Stafford that it can be trusted with children. After all, children belong within the 'family pack', and their friends too are accepted readily. This dog is friendly towards people; it is poor training and bad treatment that make it mistrustful, and cause a guarded response.

THE GUARDING STAFFORD

Much of the criticism directed towards the Stafford has no factual basis. Its character is essentially that of a lively house dog, fond of personal contact and friendly towards people. A dog like this can be a pleasure in a world where many factors can cause aggression in a dog with such a strong character. I hope that my reasoning has satisfied people within the world of dogs whom I have offended with my criticism of the aggressive dog – especially those who still believe a dog must fend off danger to its master, family and possessions. This belief is still deeply felt, perhaps too deeply.

Does the Stafford have no inclination toward guarding family, home and car, then? Those who feel that this is important will be pleased to know that with sensible training a Stafford can be taught to do this. However, on the whole, a dog which is not aggressive is far better suited to today's environment than the guard dogs of yesterday.

THE STAFFORD WITH OTHER DOGS

The Stafford may be friendly, kind, not easily upset in everyday life or by meeting people; but how does it react when meeting other animals, especially other dogs? This is a difficult question to answer. It is true that in

A comprehensive programme of socialisation will result in a calm, friendly dog.

the past they were bred so that they would fight to the bitter end: such selective breeding can go deep. I have described the development of the Stafford in detail in order to explain the instinct which lies dormant in the breed. But dog-fighting has been illegal now for over 150 years and different selection factors have come to the fore, so these temperament problems are no longer so pronounced. Sensible breeders are always trying to improve the Stafford's amiable attributes by employing careful breeding programmes: aggressive dogs should never be used. Through careful breeding, defects in the breed's social behaviour have been reduced, but they have yet to be eliminated.

THE IMPORTANCE OF SOCIAL CONTACT

The legacy of the fighting dog has resulted in a unique dog in terms of character: I know no other breed which is an all-purpose dog and suits our time so well as the Stafford, when blessed with a good temperament. The fighting instinct must, through planned training, be controlled; from the earliest age, a Stafford puppy must experience intensive social contact with its human family, littermates and other animals. Dogs are social creatures and they learn the pecking order and correct pack behaviour at an early age. It is the duty of every breeder and owner of Staffords to rear them so that they are absolutely reliable with other dogs. The first signs of aggression should be forestalled without exception, and firmly. It is unpleasant, bad for the breed and unjustifiable to be faced with Staffords at shows which show aggression towards each other; it is a gross and unforgivable training deficiency.

IGNORANT OWNERS

Unfortunately, the Stafford still attracts people with their own illusions, who need to compensate for their own failings. To turn a Stafford against other animals and to make it aggressive towards people is not hard,

Aggression should never be encouraged.

but can incur so much damage – for the owners, their environment, and the good name of the breed. We can only too easily see the reaction of the media (television, radio, newspapers etc.) to the accidents involving such dogs. Sadly, the campaign against dogs has reached a high level: in Germany the local councils, and even the President of the Animal Welfare, have demanded that the breeding of 'fighting' dogs be prohibited. Such suggestions illustrate the general lack of knowledge about the true

temperament of these dogs; and it is the very people whose training and handling of their dogs falls so far short of what is acceptable who are responsible for these campaigns.

I will end this chapter with a salutary story. I met a charming couple who were looking for a family dog, a Staffordshire Bull Terrier. They wanted to see some first, so they travelled to an international dog show, where they met some proud Stafford owners. On being asked how they behaved, one stupid owner answered: 'It kills everything!' Such owners are deadly for the breed: we can hardly be surprised when 'misunderstandings' about Staffords occur.

THE FULL LIFE

The Stafford expert W.M. Morley describes typical features of the breed: affectionate towards people and readily adaptable.

In the USA, we find this characteristic, lively description of the Stafford temperament from Linda Barker in *The Staffordshire Bull Terrier in America* (1986):

"A final note: the excitement of owning the best pure-bred dog in the world awaits you. Words cannot describe the countless hours of joy and fun that lie ahead. You will look forward to having your Stafford join you in that favourite evening chair. You will delight at your Stafford's total inability to contain its energy, while you fumble to remove its lead at the beach. Once freed it will explode with enthusiasm. It will race off, only to return again and again with a grin and an abundance of exuberant body language revealing its joy in the things it wants to share with you on the road ahead. From the time it awakens in the morning until the quiet of night, a Stafford lives life to the full."

4 BUYING A STAFFORD

Generally, when one buys a dog, it becomes a member of the family for anything up to ten or twelve years. It is therefore essential that the whole family plays a part in deciding on the right time to buy a dog, which breed to have and which puppy to choose; these decisions should not be made to suit just one member of the family. With the acquisition of a dog, a new family member is accepted for many years to come and everybody will share the good and bad times. Taking on a dog can give a lot of fun but it also entails responsibility and hard work.

When choosing a dog there is the 'love at first sight' approach, which, just as in human experience, can be a stroke of luck resulting in a harmonious relationship; but a more down-to-earth relationship, certainly one with fewer pitfalls, is likely when attraction to a particular dog is combined with a sensible planning of life ahead together. When breeders discuss buying a dog with the prospective owners they have a responsibility both to the family and to the dog to advise against it if the two are unsuited. This is especially true today, when there are many circumstances in which a dog cannot be integrated into a household. Factors concerning the owners's jobs, home, environment and family may necessitate a firm 'No'.

PARTNERS FOR LIFE

It cannot be emphasised too often that dogs are social beings and need a lifetime relationship to develop fully. It is less important whether their partners have two or four legs than that they should be there for life. We have often had young people as guests whose dearest wish was to own a dog. It would have been a pleasure to let them have one of ours in the right circumstances, but I shall always

remember with horror the story of Nathan, an exceptionally promising young male we sold to an eighteen-year-old girl. Our first impression was positive; her parents had had Bull Terriers for many years and she got on well with all of our dogs. Only later did we find out that she did not live with her parents any more: she had a two-roomed flat, and there were no parents to look after Nathan when she went to work. When we eventually discovered this it was too late: the dog had suffered irreparable damage during his isolation. We rehoused him five times and although the last owner persevered for two years he had to be destroyed – his early environment and rearing had made him impossible. This experience and others lead me to say categorically that under no circumstances should a single working person take on a young dog. In extreme cases, and only with a buyer who will put the dog first at all times, an older dog might possibly be a suitable companion.

Similarly, it is unfortunate, but working married couples should also dispense with thoughts of owning a dog. It is cruel to isolate a puppy, whether in a flat or a kennel complete with run. Recent research shows that mental development in a young dog results from its varied experiences, which stimulate its mind. It is only through the continuous absorption of new experiences that character and intelligence will develop. Neither an empty flat nor the most comfortable of kennels can offer the new experiences necessary for healthy mental development.

QUALITY TIME

Many experts describe both young and old dogs as 'terrible time-wasters'. They do take up a lot of time, but they need it, a great deal of it. The positive side is that during this time dogs can give great pleasure in return.

It may come as a surprise to the novice if I say that less time is needed to care for two dogs, but the explanation is quite simple. Two dogs already constitute a social unit; they can develop to a certain extent by their social contact with each other. It is,

Staffords that are reared together may be closer to one another than to their owner.

however, important to realise that on the whole two dogs (or more) will be closer to one another than to their owner. If the owner understands and accepts this, then looking after several dogs can indeed be less time-consuming, but the need for plenty of space is still critical: two-roomed flats are not for growing or adult Staffords. Two hours a day is a sensible period to spend with dogs, and this is possible when several dogs are kept. But again, I must advise anybody against keeping dogs if time is at a premium. The amount of time spent with a dog is of far greater importance than all other considerations. If the owner has enough time available, then there are always ways to make a dog's life more interesting.

If puppies are bred in a home environment, socialisation can begin at the earliest possible stage.

BUYING FROM A BREEDER

Where should one buy a Stafford? I think seven- to eight-week-old puppies should only be bought from their breeder, which is, in any case, the surest way of getting a pleasant dog that can be integrated into the community at the right moment. In a subsequent section about buying an adult Stafford, I discuss exceptions to this, but here I shall concentrate on buying from a breeder.

Any prospective dog owner should visit at least three or four breeders of the breed in question. It will give a clear picture of how much they care about their animals and the quality of their stock, and a visit of this kind should be undertaken a few weeks before a puppy is purchased, even if a breeder has no puppies available. It will become clear that there is a large difference between breeders. There are breeders who live for and with their dogs and those who live from them. It is better to buy from the former, although there are responsible people who work hard for their dogs and also make a living out of them.

Be careful of the breeder who will not show you all of his stock. He may only present you with one puppy: this breeder should not be the one of your choice. There are, it is true, breeders who have a hygiene craze and see every visitor as a health risk to their dogs, but this is scarcely an adequate excuse because normal breeding stock should have sufficient immunity to withstand such an ordinary occurrence as meeting people. The breeder who proudly shows off his animals and kennel facilities, along with the real nature of his Staffords, is the one I would recommend.

EARLY PUPPY DEVELOPMENT

Every prospective buyer should be aware of the possibility that the character of a seven-week-old puppy may already have suffered. This could happen if the breeder has not, as is sensible, spent enough time with it as it was growing. Further digression on this topic would be excessive here, but I recommend every prospective puppy owner to read the in-depth work on behavioural research by Eberhard Trumler. Trumler details exactly how the breeder can influence the development of a puppy's temperament between the three and seven weeks before it leaves. Breeders who through lack of time, laziness or disinterest do not spend much time with their puppies are useless at any kind of efficient dog breeding. It is better to buy a puppy from a breeder whose dog may not have had too many wins but who will do anything for the growing youngsters. The breeder with first-class breeding stock

Watch the puppies playing together to get an idea of their individual personalities.

who spends a great deal of time with puppies is the one to go for. Once a buyer has decided on a litter, he or she should visit the puppy between four and seven weeks of age as often as possible to watch its mental and physical development.

DOG OR BITCH?

Which is most suitable, a dog or a bitch? Many people are biased when faced with this question and many offer opinions which have no basis in fact. Over the past forty years I have had both dogs and bitches as my companions but even so I cannot say which I would recommend. As far as I am concerned, the decision between them is one of preference, as is a choice of colour (a good dog is never the wrong colour – a fact believed by the old breeders). There are exceptionally good dogs and bitches and this alone should be the deciding factor. It is not always the case that males are more robust, more self-confident and courageous, and neither are bitches more loving, more sensitive and loyal. From my experience I find that males are more devoted to women and bitches to men but there are always exceptions. Hygiene is no longer a major consideration because nowadays the bitch's season can be controlled and does not present problems in the home. My advice to anyone choosing

Weigh up the pros and cons when choosing whether you want a dog or a bitch. This is litter brother and sister Eclypstaff Man Machine and Eclypstaff No Regrets, co-owned by Sharon Pearce and Mr S. Horsman, bred by Mr & Mrs M. Davis.

between a dog and a bitch is to make a decision based on their physical advantages or disadvantages.

SELECTING A LITTER

In the chapter on breeding I try to define priorities for the breeder: a good breeding programme should work towards achieving health, intelligence, performance and looks. A prospective buyer should also choose a puppy based on these requirements, in that order, and then any further decisions can be made according to

71

Find out as much as possible about the puppies' parents and grandparents before making your choice.

personal preference. If selecting with the Breed Standard in mind, it must be remembered that one cannot have everything in life, and the Breed Standard shows the *ideal*; but the ideal, where all features are perfect in the same animal, has yet to be achieved. Therefore, when choosing a puppy, a certain amount of latitude is recommended.

The quality of the puppy's parents should also be considered when deciding on a litter. Do not be swayed by the list of show titles: on the Continent particularly, lack of competition at shows leads to inferior-

quality dogs achieving Championship titles. It is more important that the Stafford's parent are fearless and solid. It would be even better to know about the looks and temperament of the grandparents. How the quality of these ancestors affects the puppy is explained in my book *The Technique of Dog Breeding*.

QUESTIONS OF HEALTH
Returning to the question of health, in general the Stafford has no breed-related problems. Occasionally cleft palates occur, which arise from the Bulldog ancestry. This is fatal and the

affected puppies will die in the first few days. Cryptorchidism also occurs, and in my opinion is not uncommon in the Stafford. Another hereditary defect, which fortunately does not appear very often, was present in some lines when Stafford breeding began in Germany: those affected were termed 'swimmers' and this condition also stems from Bulldog ancestry. During the first few days of their lives 'swimmers' have a completely sunken chest; the affected puppy always lies on its tummy and later has problems getting onto its legs. But it is reasonable to say that the Stafford is basically free of hereditary defects,

including hip dysplasia (HD), which is quite common in certain breeds. Health, therefore, should not present a problem.

BAD MOTHERS

One important point is that bad mothers occur in Bull Terriers more than in other breeds, often as a result of bad selection on the part of the breeder. These bitches do not care for or nurse their puppies properly and are even aggressive with them. It is essential that a litter of Staffords is carefully watched over by the breeder during the first few weeks to avoid any accidents the mother may cause,

A sound temperament is essential when choosing breeding stock. This is Kecila Black Opel with her 8-week-old son Mincol True Grit.

including lying on the puppies. If one wishes to buy a Stafford bitch to breed, look at the mother's behaviour. Even better, also find out about the behaviour of the previous generation. I hope that through carefully planned selection we shall be able to produce Staffords with good nursing instincts who are good mothers.

ASSESSING THE PUPPIES

I have already mentioned that the breeder and his family need to spend a great deal of time with the puppies: this is very important. Well-reared puppies will be friendly and ready for a game with anyone. A puppy that is scared of strangers in its own pen or lethargically sits in a corner is best avoided. As I am not an expert at picking a puppy from a litter, I shall turn to the advice of two experts, experienced Stafford specialists with many years' experience in the breed, whose comments will be helpful.

John F. Gordon, an experienced Stafford breeder, suggests that careful observation should be made of the temperament of the puppies and their behaviour towards strangers, and recommends friendly dogs. He says that good bone structure should be looked for, where bones are round and strong, and points out that by seven weeks of age the puppies should have good round rib cages. Splayed feet are

The breeder will help you to make an expert evaluation.

undesirable. Gordon reminds intending buyers to look at puppies from the front and the side, the better to assess the depth and width of the muzzle, as well as the depth of the top of the head, shortness of muzzle and breadth of the top of the head: there should be definite prominent cheeks, and cheek muscles should be visible.

Gordon further states that puppies examined from the side should look square, like a cart-horse: a firm topline is desirable, with a short tail and the elbows tucked well in and the feet should not be overly turned out. He is insistent that the movement of puppies should be observed; there should not be any stiffness in their walk, no hopping movements. Ears, he admits, are difficult. Puppies with prick ears should be avoided, similarly those with half-erect ears; both will fail to develop into rose ears. A small ear is desirable, with delicate ear tissue. The correct rose ear folds towards the back, showing a little of the inside of the ear.

CHECKING THE ANCESTORS

Michael D. Vergino also comments on the selection of a puppy in *The Staffordshire Bull Terrier in America*. He advises that, when selecting a puppy from a litter, it is advisable to check both parents and if possible also the grandparents, particularly because, if the puppy is to be used for breeding, it is important to see if line breeding to good ancestors has been carried out and, if possible, the extent of in-breeding. He also stresses the importance of visiting the litter from four weeks onwards, advising that the final choice should be made by the time the puppies are seven weeks old but when the whole litter is still together.

THE PUPPY HEAD

Vergino goes on to say that the head of a seven-week-old puppy should appear very big, relative to its body. A short muzzle should be looked for, giving an impression of strength. When viewed from the side, a noticeable stop is important. Puppies with long muzzles in proportion to the rest of the head are not recommended. Looking down at the head, the muzzle should be broad but narrowing slightly towards the nose. At this age many wrinkles on the face are normal; Vergino speaks of an 'accordion' effect. The folds indicate that the head has space to grow. However, if these wrinkles appear excessive, then one should ask about the development of the parents and grandparents and how they grew out of theirs. Folds in an adult dog are undesirable.

It is important that the ears are set far back on the side of the head. High-set ears are undesirable; they will not fold as rose ears and may later become pricked. It is important that the ears appear thin and small: if they are already folded as rose ears it is virtually certain that they will remain so for the rest of the dog's life.

THE PUPPY'S MOUTH

The puppy's teeth should be checked and should make a scissor bite. Michael Vergino warns against breeders who assure that a faulty bite will be corrected as the dog grows older. A slightly overshot bite with the top teeth well in front of the lower can be forgiven at the age of seven weeks, as this can improve with time, but puppies who are already undershot do not alter sufficiently. It should be remembered that the Stafford has a tendency to be undershot, an inheritance from its Bulldog ancestors. The undershot mouth is characterised by a lower jaw which is longer than the upper jaw. It is unlikely that an undershot, seven-week-old puppy will develop a normal bite, and at this age the fault should be considered serious. It is important to notice a wry mouth, where the incisors of the upper and lower jaw are not in line with each other: this fault will not correct itself with time.

THE EYES

The eye placement in a Stafford is very important and will influence its whole appearance. At seven weeks old, eyes that are close together, small or almond-shaped should be avoided. The eyes should be round, set wide apart and ideally of medium size. It is difficult to judge the colour of the eyes in young puppies. When they first open they are light in colour and they begin to darken from three weeks onwards. However, if the eyes are still light by twelve weeks of age, little subsequent change in colour can be expected.

THE BODY

The structure of a puppy's body should give an impression of much strength but must also be well balanced without exaggeration in any one feature.

When viewed from above, the neck should be narrower than the head, then broaden into the shoulders; it should be of medium length, neither too long nor too short. The bones of a Stafford puppy should be strong, and are a good indication of the type of Stafford it will grow into: the terrier types are light-boned and Bulldog types are often heavy.

It is important that a puppy has a good spring of rib, with well-tucked-in elbows. If viewed from above, the elbows should not stick out but be pressed close in.

A good back on a puppy is straight and short, neither dipping nor roached. It is common to find a roached back and upright shoulders in the same specimen and both are hard to breed out. When viewing a puppy from the side, the chest must reach below the elbows. If the chest is not of good depth at seven weeks then the dog will tend to be long-legged. If, on the other hand, the chest is too deep

Occasionally a puppy is born with a screw tail, which is a throwback to the breed's Bulldog ancestry.

(a result of its Bulldog ancestry), the adult dog will quite possibly be short in the leg. This is why it is so important that the chest and legs be in correct proportion. Viewed from the front the legs should be perfectly straight with the feet only turning out slightly. The pasterns should not show any signs of weakness. The hind legs when viewed from the rear must also be straight, neither cow-hocked nor bow-legged. Viewed from the side the knee should be well turned and the hocks be short and low to the ground.

It may be helpful to refer to the drawings included with the Standard to appreciate these comments. It is interesting to compare what can already be seen in the puppy with that desired in the Standard.

OTHER IMPORTANT POINTS
The puppy's tail should be set on low and not be too long. It will tend to carry its tail quite high at a young age, but this can change as it grows. The puppy's feet must be compact at this stage; splayed feet are often an inherited fault and the parents should also be examined.

Healthy puppies have fairly rounded tummies as with most baby animals. A seven-week-old puppy cannot be expected to have the same tummy shape as the adult.

The choice of colour is mainly a question of personal preference. As long as the colour abides by the rules of the Standard (black and tan or liver is undesirable), then it makes no difference in the show ring.

Good pigmentation is important. The puppies as well as the adults should have dark claws, eye rims and noses. It is especially important to note the pigmentation on white dogs. White dogs with little pigmentation often suffer from allergies and other skin ailments.

The experts quite rightly emphasise the point that buying a good puppy is not easy and no recommendations can guarantee a top-class specimen. Take along a breed expert when choosing a puppy: it is important to look for good points in the puppy, and any fool can find faults, whereas the real experts can see the merits.

THE NATURE OF PUPPIES
To end, here is Linda Barker on *How to survive a puppy*:

"Staffordshire Bull Terrier puppies can be the bane of your existence or the delight of your life. They chew when teething, eat a little bit at a time, and, just as often, they find the need to relieve themselves when and where the mood strikes. They will want to play when it is least convenient, and are always asleep when you want them to show off for guests. At the same time they are destroying their surroundings. Stafford puppies can be enchantingly 'cute'. Watching these little dynamos romp and run about the yard and stage their mock battles can

keep you smiling all day. In fact, only the mud-caked smile of a Stafford puppy running to you with the news that your rose garden has been undermined could dissolve your anger.

"Raising a puppy is work, especially if you take the time to raise it properly. Puppies, like children, must learn acceptable behaviour. It is here that the burden of responsibility falls upon you. Time, patience and common sense are your allies. What a puppy learns in the first six months of its life establishes the pattern for later behaviour."

BUYING AN OLDER DOG
It is common to find potential buyers who argue that they can better judge the merits of an older dog than a puppy. This is of course true as far as the exterior of the animal goes, but it does not take into consideration how the dog has developed mentally. It is a scientifically proven fact that a puppy of seven to nine weeks old can be well integrated into family life by caring owners without any upset. Not many people realise that, in the wild, puppies are brought up by the father from the age of seven weeks – this seems to be the acceptable (and successful) time in a wild pack.

It is also unusual to find a really promising youngster for sale, for reasons which are easy to understand.

A sensible breeder is pleased if one of his puppies develops into a very good young animal. This is not always a certainty, for a whole series of faults may appear, but if one does have the good luck to rear a good dog, why should one want to sell it? It would surely take a good deal of money to break such a successful relationship. On the whole, young or adult Staffords are only offered for sale if the owner has made mistakes in the animal's rearing or if the dog has not fulfilled the owner's expectations. Anatomical faults may also be found in such animals. Probably more than eighty per cent of dogs between three and eighteen months offered for sale are a disappointment in some way or other to their owners. There are, of course many people who do not possess the ability to rear a puppy properly, and possibly some dogs that are offered for sale may well have developed differently in the hands of sensible owners.

At six months of age, a puppy has already been exposed to many influential experiences.

UNDERSTANDING PUPPY DEVELOPMENT

Behavioural research has clearly demonstrated that a puppy's ability to learn different things is related to its development, and an understanding of this is necessary for the sensible upbringing of a young dog. It has also been shown that if these stages are not recognised at the right time, learning abilities can be lost and the young dog will be mentally backward. Suitable training during these stages can be neglected by the first owner of a dog, and, if this has happened, even an expert second owner will have problems trying to educate the dog.

Similarly, if the anatomical development of a young dog has suffered during these stages, then the resulting faults will also be difficult to correct. Rickets and overtreatment with vitamins are examples: both will damage the bone structure of a growing dog and can seldom be corrected by subsequent improvements in diet. The same goes for overexercise: if a dog's first owner overexercises it continually this may cause damage to the tendons and ligaments, and even the greatest of care in the future will not remedy the problem.

People can be angered by the faults caused in a dog by its first owner and it is often difficult for new owners to put up with the resulting problems. For all these reasons, if it is possible, introduce a puppy into the home rather than an older dog. There are puppies, young adults and even well-known dogs for sale due to special circumstance, but even in 'special circumstances', the dog might still suffer damage caused by the ignorance of the first owner.

Of course, there are also personal problems which necessitate the sale of an older dog, for instance death, divorce, moving to a flat or abroad etc. I was once lucky enough to buy a beautiful and very good bitch as a result of the owner's divorce. I had previously tried to buy her a year before, and I was delighted with her. She became our best brood bitch and

gave us a great deal of pleasure but, along with all her attributes, she brought faults caused by her first owners and these we could not eradicate. In spite of the positive effects on my kennel and the international Championships she won for us, we have learnt from this experience and have never again bought a fully mature dog.

TRIAL PERIODS FOR OLDER DOGS

One of my favourites was a young male who won my heart with his charm and lovable temperament. I did so want him when I met him at eight months. He looked a very promising young animal, and he certainly did turn out well. I saw him over several days while staying with his breeder, and he was just my cup of tea. I would have bought him except for the fact that the breeder did not want him to leave the country, but the only reason I would have bought a dog of his age was because I was able fully to assess his temperament, and it was just to my liking. The dog and I got to know each other, especially on our walks. Compared to a puppy, I could determine so much more in this older dog and everything was just right.

Anyone wanting to buy a young dog or adult Stafford should take time to study the dog carefully and, if possible, both parents. It is in the best interests of the prospective buyer, owner and dog to agree on a trial period for adjustment, and four weeks is a reasonable time. It is best to try to live with the new addition to the family and to see if the dog can be integrated. This kind of sale requires trust between the buyer and the seller, both wanting to do what is right for the dog. This is especially true of someone with a very good animal to sell, who will be even more determined that the dog ends up in the right hands. Prospective buyers who ask for such a trial period should be welcomed.

There are, unfortunately, buyers who use a trial period for testing the 'hardness' and 'sharpness' or even 'fighting drive' of the dog. Anyone confronted with this sort of person should strenuously discourage them: the trial period is for getting the dog to settle into its new surroundings in peace without 'courage tests' or any other such experiments. A sensible buyer will appreciate the seller who is very cautious before a entrusting a well-loved dog into his care.

What happens to all the young dogs who litter the market because of the mistakes made by their owners or breeders? Where should they go? I cannot answer this – responsibility lies with the breeders. It depends whether the potential buyer of such a dog is

A trial period should be used to give the dog a chance to settle into his new surroundings.

prepared to put up with the inherited or acquired defects for the following ten years or more. True affection towards such a dog – love at first sight – may, despite the dog's bad start, provide it with a happy new home, which would be the best possible 'happy ending'. However, the fact of the matter is that buying an older dog does involve greater risk than the acquisition of a seven-week-old puppy from a good breeder.

5 LIVING WITH A STAFFORD

It is a fact that the Stafford has evolved in the Black Country as an all-purpose dog and it requires little special care and attention. Staffords are not specially demanding but, like all bull breeds, they need a great deal of human companionship. They are equally at home in a flat or a small house; in a flat they are quiet dogs, but outside full of energy. Properly trained, the Stafford is an easy-going, family dog which will give few problems.

Jack Barnard's ideas on the phases of development in a young dog include special attention to the basically friendly character of the Stafford and its great intelligence. He comments that the intelligence of the adult Stafford is exceptionally high, though he adds that it takes eighteen to twenty-four months before the dog has grown up. A twelve-month-old Stafford may not appear very clever but after this time its mental development is very fast. I have indicated elsewhere that I believe intelligence in a Stafford is largely dependent on its owner; Staffords take a long time to mature, and the experts emphasise that their physical development can take up to three years.

THE SAFE GARDEN

If the dog has the chance to run freely in the garden, it should be remembered that it is not a dog that will potter around. It will get bored in its own territory and any exciting occurrences outside can be tempting, therefore sensible fencing is necessary to keep it in. Do not underestimate this little athlete: the Stafford's ability to jump is incredible – a fence of 1.8 m high is recommended. Also, all Terriers have great curiosity and can discover the smallest of holes in a fence. A fence with a rabbit-proof lower half and an upper part of a larger mesh is a good solution. It should be dug at least 20 cm deep into the ground so that, if the dog tries to dig under the fence, it will be confronted by yet more wire. If it is not possible to dig the fence in, then some tight mesh can be dug into the ground and attached to the fence above.

Care must be taken to ensure garden plants are 'dog-friendly'. There are some plants and bushes in gardens that are poisonous to dogs, including laburnum, azalea, some cherry trees, rhododendrons and mistletoe, to mention just a few. A flower or vegetable garden can be fenced off from the area the dog is allowed to use, being for humans only.

DOG CAGES

In my home we do not use dog baskets, although they look attractive. Dogs are naturally cave dwellers and need a type of cave to sleep in. For many years I have used cages; the dog likes being able to sit inside with an old blanket and perhaps a toy, and has a feeling of security. The lockable door is also useful for young dogs as they can be locked in, and thus prevented from eating electric cables, carpets and furniture when not being watched. In a cage, a dog can gnaw a bone without making a mess on the carpet, etc. Staffords have very strong teeth and jaws which need to be used, especially

Make sure that all the plants in your garden are dog-friendly.

when they are very young and before the second teeth have come through. Rather than ruin good furniture, it is cheaper to buy a cage than have to replace it. Dogs will soon get used to sleeping in a cage, and it is also useful on journeys and in hotels. In a car, a

The crate is a valuable training aid, but should not be misused.

cage is safer for dog, driver and other passengers.

EXERCISE

A major consideration in looking after a Stafford is the correct exercise. Young dogs in any breed tend to be overexercised by their owners in the first five to six months of life. Behaviour studies of wild dog families have proved that parents take great care to ensure their young are not overtired during the first month; this is a period during which play and rest are alternated for the good of the puppies' mental and physical development. It is very engaging to see a twelve-week-old puppy walking on a lead along the road or at shows,

but although it is in a young puppy's nature to follow its leader, and it will do so willingly, it is wrong to let it. Too much exercise at a young age may cause permanent skeletal and/or ligament damage; short daily exercise is quite enough when combined with a game. This does not go against making sure that a young dog gets as much contact with its own kind as possible. Simply, it is common sense to avoid overtiring a puppy of only a few months old at an age when all its bones, ligaments and muscles are very soft and need time to harden and tighten. Long walks for puppies up to the age of four months are forbidden; walks should only gradually increase in duration and distance after that age. By eight months, the puppy will be able to manage a human walk.

A growing youngster should be played with a great deal. It can be taught to retrieve and play tug-of-war. There is no proof of the latter ruining the dentition of a puppy; it is only an excuse for faults arising from the dog's breeding. A young dog needs games to exercise its muscles and give it mental stimulation, but after every game a rest should be allowed. Playing and resting are equally important for a dog's mental and physical development.

Assuming a young puppy has been sensibly reared to a seven-month-old

84

A youngster may seem to have boundless energy but it is important not to overexercise.

'hooligan', then the question of exercise comes into its own. J.F. Gordon emphasises the need for a healthy Stafford to have plenty of exercise so that its body can develop properly. A Stafford is quite capable of six times the amount of exercise its owner can manage on a normal walk. In traffic a Stafford must be on a lead, as all dogs should be, and I strongly advise against experiments. Every year, too many dogs are victims of the carelessness of their owners. There is plenty of opportunity out in the fields and woods for running off the lead. If time is limited, then it is useful to teach the dog to retrieve: a good ball game can be equivalent of a long walk on the lead of more than a mile.

USING A LEAD
On the whole, experienced breeders in England advise daily walks on the lead of about three miles for a young, growing Stafford of more than eight to nine months. This is called roadwork, but it is not always continuous: a good rest at intervals is

Do not let your dog pull when he is walking on the lead.

necessary. My own feeling is that these walks should be varied, which is better for both dog and owner. Taking a Stafford out on a bicycle certainly makes sense considering the relatively greater amount of exercise that results. For exercise like this, the dog should be taught to trot alongside the bicycle, not to gallop; this trot should be a faster version of the slow trot. The dog should be kept on a lead while being exercised by bicycle, the lead being held in the left hand. It must not be overtaxed with this form of training, and should not attempt it before ten months old.

Some breeders recommend walking a Stafford on asphalt to toughen the pads of the feet and keep the nails short. No dog should pull while on the lead: it must hang loosely between the dog and owner. If a dog is allowed to pull, the ligaments and joints in the shoulder and knees will be overtaxed and could become overstretched. It is also not a pleasure for the owner to be pulled through the streets. It is important to remember that the daily walk should not only be undertaken in fine weather but on rainy days too, although the dog will need a good rubdown afterwards. Nor should the important principle of not overexercising be forgotten.

DEVELOPMENT THROUGH PLAY
The possibilities of exercise with a ball in an open field are many, and a game with a strong stick can give a dog a lot of fun. It can be a real pleasure to see what can be done with a Stafford who will retrieve a ball, especially in a hilly area, where many happy games can be played with a dog. A Stafford can also take large obstacles in its stride.

A growing Stafford needs to play games so that he can exercise both his mind and his body.

On my visit to Bill Hodgkinson in the Black Country, I watched the traditional method of developing the muscles of a Stafford with an old car tyre. A Stafford loves to play with its strength, and this plainly gives real pleasure. Old car tyres are not obligatory. A German-bred Stafford, Dodger, liked to jump for the highest branches of a tree, grab them and swing. He much enjoyed testing the tree's resistance to his concentrated demolition work. In Sweden I met a complete Stafford family where the patched father, also on a visit, played happily with the brood bitch's family of four nine-week-old puppies. Similarly, on a visit to the Domestic Animals Research Station at Wolfswinkel to see Eberhard Trumler, I saw a dog family which demonstrated the best possible social behaviour with happy, wild games followed by rest.

There are many different ways in which a Stafford can use its athletic body; but as well as playing wild games they also enjoy spending hours on the settee or as lap dogs. This broad range of activities and behaviour gives the Stafford owner endless new experiences.

COAT CARE

'Easy-care': this is a guarantee that can be used without fail to describe a

A brisk rubdown should be all that is necessary for the maintenance of a Stafford's coat.

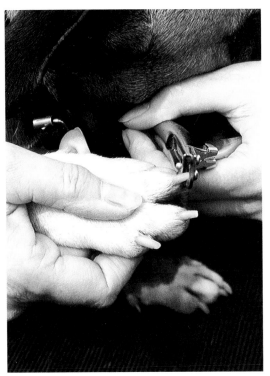

Nails should wear down through roadwork, but, if necessary, they can be trimmed with nail-clippers.

It is important to check that teeth and gums are clean and healthy.

Stafford. They are short-haired dogs and in contrast to many other breeds there is nothing to 'cut off', not from the ears, tail or coat. So even when a Stafford decides to run through muddy water or charge across boggy cow pasture, a clean-water rinse is all that is necessary. Many caring Stafford owners brush their dogs every day or at least twice a week, but I know of many Staffords who never get brushed and yet feel good and have a shiny coat; I hardly ever brush my Bull

Terriers. The quality of a dog's coat depends to a large extent on the right food.

After a walk in snow or rain the only attention a Stafford's coat needs is to dry it with a towel. A floor cloth is very useful: any dirt in the coat can be removed by repeatedly washing and rinsing the cloth. This is all that is needed for a perfect, well-cared-for coat.

Claws on a Stafford should be walked down naturally in roadwork.

A puppy of seven weeks needs to be fed four times a day.

Care of eyes and ears is the same for the Stafford as for any other breed. One problem that may occur in heavy dogs, if they sleep on hard floors, is pressure sores, but if the cage is well padded with blankets or towels, or the dog has convinced itself that the sofa is the best place, then these should not occur. If they do, then Vaseline twice a day is the best treatment, and this will keep the affected areas supple so that they do not dry out or crack.

FEEDING
The right food is essential and, together with suitable exercise, will shape the dog – not forgetting

inherent hereditary factors. Today's accepted feeding practice indicates that most breeders believe in 'less is more'. Too often dogs are overfed because owners take no notice of the basic rule which states that a slim dog is a healthy dog. Unfortunately, some Stafford owners believe that substance is quality, and this has resulted in crazes such as the administration of anabolic steroids, which are intended to make the dog heavier. The Stafford Standard demands a well-muscled dog, but at the same time a solid dog. Fat is not muscle. Muscles produced by anabolic steroids constitute premeditated bodily harm to your own dog!

A Stafford must not be overfed. Dog food manufacturers recommend suitable quantities of their products and these can be followed in good faith. Nevertheless, a dog's diet should be varied. A puppy at the age of seven weeks is fed four times a day; from three months on, this is reduced to three meals a day and from six months, two meals are quite sufficient. By the time the dog is twelve months old, it can be fed on one meal a day without any complications. Our adult dogs are offered the following variations:

Day 1: About 1lb (500 grams) raw meat, plus grated vegetables and a handful of flakes soaked in hot water.

Day 2: ¼ lb (120 grams) quark mixed with about 1pt (500 ml) yoghurt plus a handful of flakes or oat flakes, and added to this some grape sugar, honey and fruits.

Day 3: Complete dog food with some hot rich meat or bone juice poured over it.

Day 4: A tin of dog food from one of the leading brands.

This varied diet can be repeated in a four-day cycle on a regular basis. Puppies can have basically the same mixture of food but in smaller quantities and divided into four meals. Puppies and young dogs should also receive daily doses of calcium and one teaspoonful of cod liver oil. The calcium content in different preparations is not necessarily the same. I have bought food with no added vitamins and supplemented with the recommended dose of Canovel and have always achieved good results.

To feed sensibly, the most important principle is to remove anything a dog has not eaten within five minutes and not to offer it again before the next feed is due. Too many dog owners do not adhere to this rule, and it is the cause of many bad eaters. If a dog eats its food in a certain time with no fuss, then it is getting the right amount. If anything is left, less should be offered for the next feed. If a dog keeps licking the bowl for some time afterwards then more should be offered at the next feed. Dogs should not be given anything in between meals, although I do give them two dog cakes at bedtime as a treat.

The owner should not allow the dog to become choosy by always giving its favourite dish, which is likely to be meat. It is the owner's duty to provide a balanced diet: variation should ensure that the dog has healthy and nutritious food. Large bones are welcome work for a dog and its teeth, but do not give chicken or pork bones because they splinter and if they are swallowed then these sharp fragments can cause untold internal damage. Pork should not be given, whether raw or cooked. The best meat is beef, mutton or lamb;

venison is also acceptable as is dry meat. Proper meat is best, but tripe can also be given. Other internal organs may be given, but care should be taken when feeding spleen, livers or melts as these may not only accumulate environmental pollutants but can also, eaten in large quantities, cause diarrhoea. I do not recommend lungs because I think they have little nutritional value.

WORMING AND VACCINATIONS

All young dogs must be wormed. The breeder should already have wormed the puppies at least twice before they are sold and another worming course should follow four weeks later. Any good, well-tested proprietary brand can be used and the experts recommend three-monthly courses until the dog is one year old. Older dogs do not, on the whole, suffer from roundworms; if worms are a concern, then a faeces test can be carried out by the veterinary surgeon, as it is important not to give worming remedies unless it is known what type of worms the dog has.

Regular inoculations against distemper, leptospirosis, hepatitis and parvovirus (and rabies on the continent) must be given without fail. Those who have seen the terrible effects of canine distemper will appreciate how important these inoculations are. The veterinary surgery should not be visited for trifling matters, as infections can be picked up in the waiting room. However, it is advisable to watch out for indications of ill health such as lack of appetite and high temperature, both very good warning signs. The normal temperature of a dog is around 38.5 degrees C; anything above 39.2 degrees C should be watched very carefully.

THE INDOOR DOG

The Stafford has a short coat and so should not be kept outside. It is unreasonable to breed these ideal, short-coated house dogs and then keep them outside in draughty kennels! The worst thing about keeping dogs in kennels is the mental damage it can cause: there is nothing wrong with keeping a dog in a good kennel for a few hours, but to be permanently shut away is nothing short of cruelty.

THE VETERAN

Whatever the breed, dogs should be able to grow old and remain healthy and good family companions for a long time. A vital mark of quality in a breed is the healthy old dogs, where breeding, rearing, care and feeding have been well carried out. Such dogs are a credit to their owners.

High-quality care will help your dog to live to a ripe old age. This is Wyrefare Tearaway Jake, aged 12 years.

TRAINING YOUR STAFFORD

What follows is an entirely new dimension in dog training, based on the results of research during the last few years. Careful observation of naturally-reared dog families has demonstrated that the dog is a social creature with many inherited behavioural patterns which make learning easy. Results suggest that two-thirds of a dog's behaviour is a consequence of its ability to learn.

THE ESTABLISHED ORDER

In the natural dog family there are no 'anti-authority' influences. The puppies are born into an established order within the dog pack; the older dogs are always dominant, and, through play, a pecking order develops between the puppies. Eberhard Trumler concludes in his work *Man and Dog* that it is wrong to assume fights occur continually to establish a hierarchy in pack groups who have developed together from puppyhood. Fights which take place for this purpose only occur between adults living together but who have not grown up together.

Trumler's observations regarding continual teaching by older animals are especially impressive. Young growing dogs need a distinct order in the family, shown by rules of play in relationships within the litter. These rules of play are determined by the older dogs who make it quite clear what form of conduct is acceptable. Human beings can do no better than to train dogs on the same principles, in what is in effect a mixed pack of dogs and men. Natural upbringing begins with three-week-old puppies being taught by the dam and, at seven weeks, the father takes over their education. There are parallels with this natural behaviour when a puppy is integrated with its new family at a similar age: the role of the new owner is then to continue the puppy's education in its new surroundings.

Previous training ideas have suggested young animals should be allowed to grow without training until about twelve months old, at which point a sort of training scheme is established. This method is outdated and has been proved wrong; it is far better to use each day of the puppy's life to teach it, through play, what is acceptable behaviour.

PUNISHMENT

An important aspect of training is how to punish in play. Forget the old wives' tale that recommends using a folded newspaper – I have never seen a wild dog chastise a puppy with a newspaper. In a dog pack it is the mouth that feeds, caresses and cleans, and which also chastises. In the wild, the mother regurgitates the predigested food from her mouth, caresses and cleans her tongue, and punishes any naughty behaviour by vigorous shaking. The voice in a dog family pack also plays an important role. If the parents want to make it clear to their growing youngsters that a bone or food is for themselves, they will issue a warning growl to teach the puppies to respect their wishes.

RECEPTIVE LEARNING PERIODS

Another important finding to emerge from the latest research is the fact that the brain of a small puppy can be likened to an unprogrammed computer. A computer can only bring forth the responses programmed into it, and the learning ability of puppies operates along similar lines. A strange phenomenon, of great importance, is that, if brain cells are programmed during their most receptive period, they remain programmed for life. If unused during this period they will waste away, never to be available for programming again. Those who consider this point will realise how important it is that a growing puppy should receive as many varied experiences as possible to provide its brain with fresh stimuli. If young dogs are isolated, they will vegetate in their boring, hygienic kennels; their ability will be stunted and most certainly they will end up as stupid animals.

The most precious investment a person can make in a dog is to spend time with it. Not too much planned training, but rather a development – exactly the course the wild dog dam, and later the father, take with their developing young. It is important to remember that a puppy should rest and not go for long walks in the first six months of its life. Otherwise, every hour spent with the growing puppy is essential to its correct mental development.

TRAINING AND THE STAFFORD CHARACTER

It is not feasible to give an in-depth account of all stages of training in this book, from house-training to heeling off the lead, and in any case there are books written solely for this purpose. A few specialised aspects of training are, however, particularly relevant to the Stafford breed. First, the Stafford can be stubborn, full of self-confidence and obstinacy. These stubborn dogs need a human partner who is consistent in his approach to training. A "No" must mean no, and remain that way, just as allowed behaviour must remain allowed. Fickleness and inconsistency are the greatest enemies of successful dog training.

Also, the Stafford is an extremely intelligent dog and can register its owner's desires, moods and complacency. Intelligent dogs discover very quickly which members of the family insist on obedience, which of them will give in if it behaves charmingly, or for whom it need not even bother to prick its ears, let alone do as it is told. A dog can work this out, and an intelligent one will enjoy doing so; the owner must exercise sensible self-control when faced with such a dog.

CURBING AGGRESSION
Other problems typical of many Staffords are the inheritance of the fighting instinct, and their quarrelsome behaviour towards other dogs. I have already discussed the changes in the social behaviour of dogs which had been bred for dog-fighting, and these changes can result in training problems. The dog bred for fighting will fight to the bitter end, rather than acquiesce to a hierarchy or determine territorial domains; these Staffords will never offer a submissive gesture, nor will they accept it from another. In another book I have described how a Bull Terrier can go beyond the 'red phase' in a fight: this red phase is something like the stage a bull reaches when it furiously reacts to red cloth, with excitement and fury surpassing all reason. Beyond this stage, a Bull Terrier feels no pain and will not give up until the bitter end.

Based on my own experience, I believe this stage can be avoided in eighty to ninety per cent of Staffords by thoughtful training, so that dog and owner never find themselves in such a situation. How is this achieved? It begins with sensible intervention by the breeder when puppies are four to five weeks old. At this age the first arguments occur and this is normal in any litter – there is nothing more important than play for a growing animal and these rough games also determine the pecking order in a litter. There is, however, a certain tone which an experienced breeder will recognise as indicating when the argument is becoming very angry, and that the puppies are approaching the red phase. The puppies' mother will also recognise it and, whereas she will ignore normal play, here she will intervene with motherly authority and part them. If a bitch ignores them altogether, then the breeder must do the intervening. From my visits to England and my twenty-five years breeding Bull Terriers, I can say that the early training of puppies contributes a great deal towards teaching a young dog to curb its aggression.

PROMOTING GOOD RELATIONSHIPS
It is very important that buyers of a Stafford puppy should do their best to offer their new companion not only

many relationships with other humans but also the opportunity to meet as many friendly dogs as possible. They will thus continue the education initiated by the dam and the breeder, and the young dog will learn to appreciate sensible relationships with its canine friends. It is essential that none of the growing dog's playmates is bad-tempered and that unpleasant encounters are avoided. However, it is perfectly normal for an older dog to put a younger one in its place, if necessary quite roughly, if the youngster does not respect its elder. Frequent encounters with other dogs and plenty of opportunities to play are the best guarantee against a young dog becoming a fighter. The owners must still play a part if their dog acts in an unfriendly manner towards others; in the wild the top dog will intervene, and similarly it is the owners' duty to protect their dog's more timid playmates who would not know how to defend themselves. Owners should let their own dog know how far it can go.

THE HOOLIGAN PHASE
In young dogs, unsocial behaviour can be expected between nine and eleven months and again around eighteen to twenty months. These are periods equivalent to the stages of puberty in human beings and it is important the 'hooligan' learns acceptable limits of behaviour. At this point, it is essential for owners to take the trouble and extra effort to find suitable playmates for their dogs. Correct social conduct can only be learnt by as much contact as possible – this is as true for animals as it is for human beings.

ADULT AGGRESSION
As for the ten to twenty per cent of Staffords who, despite a sensible upbringing, still display their fighting dog heritage, their aggression is

Be sure to curb aggression towards other dogs.

Well-trained Staffords will be calm and relaxed in each other's company.

usually aroused when an adult dog has had a bad experience through being attacked and has had to defend itself. After the first encounter the lust for the fight grows, and the once-dormant instinct is aroused. Unfortunately many Staffords will be only too willing to start a fight after such an experience. It is, therefore, important to take every opportunity to train such a dog with others; it can be kept on a lead when meeting other dogs as one way of curbing its aggression, and of course, it is advisable to keep a dog who has had a fight under careful supervision during walks. It should be called back immediately should a potentially unpleasant meeting with a strange dog arise. I have walked my dogs in parks in and around cities for many years and during these walks my dogs have met many strange dogs and made dog friends with whom they

have greatly enjoyed playing. When my dogs first meet a new dog, I am always careful to curb any aggression instantly.

STOPPING A FIGHT

What should be done if a fight does occur? Bulldogs, Staffords and Bull Terriers will exhibit a common style of fighting, characterised by them refusing to let go of their opponent. Forget the nonsense about throwing a bucket of water over the offenders or the senseless cruelty of attempting to beat the dogs, or even to get between them. These are all completely useless, can lead to injuries all round, and still do not encourage the fighters to part.

J.F. Gordon told me he had a deep water-butt at his kennel which was always kept full and, if his dogs fought, they would be thrown into it.

The fighting pair would surface once or twice together but usually by the third time they would let go, simply because they did not have enough breath left to keep hanging on. A source of deep water is ideal but is not always handy when a fight occurs.

Alternative methods rely on the same principle: dogs can be parted when they become short of breath. Experienced dog owners are aware of this and will cut off the fighting dogs' air supply by twisting their collars. There is a fashionable tradition among Staffordshire Bull Terrier owners to use broad, decorated collars: they are totally unsuitable, and are more like harnesses used to attach a dog to a cart than a sensible means for teaching lead training, let alone suitable for making a dog let go in a fight. The basic principle is that the narrower the collar, the more pressure can be applied to the neck. If a dog is being 'strangled' to stop it fighting, the best way is to make the collar dig in as deep as possible and really cut off the air supply. Those decorative but useless studded collars should be sacrificed. A Stafford should wear a round, sewn, narrow collar – not a choker, as they are not necessary and at times are not reliable; all that is needed is a good round, sewn, strong collar.

Not everyone has sufficiently strong hands to twist a dog's collar enough to cause it problems with its breathing. There is another method of parting two fighting dogs, but it must be carried out simultaneously and in three stages by both owners of their own dogs – arguing and shouting with the other dog owner must be resisted: Stage 1, grab the dog's tail and lift it so that its hind legs no longer touch the ground. This will reduce both animals' ability to fight. Stage 2, without letting go of the tail, the free hand should grip the collar and twist it to cut off the air supply. Do not try to pull the dogs apart as this only encourages them to hold on tighter. Stage 3, at a word, the dogs should be pushed together. This is a completely unexpected movement for the dogs and they will release their grip. The moment of surprise must be used, and as a rule they will let go. They should then be kept well apart to avoid grabbing each other again. If this technique does not work first time around, it surely will on the second attempt. I have parted many dogs, even with my physical disability: a certain knack develops after the first or second encounter. I hope I have not alarmed anyone with this description, but it is simply a necessary piece of knowledge for the day-to-day keeping of a dog. With luck, it will never be necessary to use it, but if ever there is a fight it will be of some help.

GUARD DOG TRAINING

There is another training problem: the Staffords' normal nature should be that of a dog friendly towards people, one which sees a stranger as a welcome change rather than a possible threat. Yet there are undoubtedly owners who would also like their dogs to be guard dogs. There are a few observations to be made on this.

Staffords as a breed tend not to bark a great deal. If a Stafford is annoyed, it will take up a typical threatening stance which strangers usually find unnerving; when a growling Stafford shows its teeth, it is usually enough to keep strangers at bay. This threatening attitude is only taken when they feel themselves or their owners are at risk.

J.F. Gordon emphasises that a young Stafford can be taught without much problem to be a good guard. A friend should be asked to make noises outside the house, perhaps by knocking on a door or window. Every normal young dog will prick up its ears and take note of this unusual sound, and more often than not the dog will bark. If not, then the owner should attempt a 'woof', after which even the most stupid of dogs will bark as well. When the dog barks, it should be praised, and the more angrily it barks, the more the praise. After a few attempts, the young dog has usually understood and begins to bark. If the dog's owner feels really threatened, then the dog can be taken to the door and encouraged to be on guard by opening the door with one hand, holding the dog with the other. This action alone should motivate the dog to adopt threatening behaviour. On the whole, these procedures should be more than adequate and any burglar would avoid taking a risk with such a dog.

In principle, owners must beware of encouraging aggressive behaviour in a young dog; it will soon get the impression that threatening behaviour pleases its master and will continue to threaten. The Stafford owner can face long-term problems as a result of inappropriate training as a guard. As the youngster grows, so will its aggressive behaviour increase, and this can turn into a nightmare for the owners. The wrong initial training results in the dog only being able to be exercised on a lead or having to be kept in a garden or kennel – a dog's life indeed.

DOG SHOWS

Is it reasonable to discuss dog shows in a chapter entitled 'Living with Staffords'? I think it is: I am, after all, dealing with a breed that has arisen due to human planning and manipulation. Pedigree dog breeding is based upon a Breed Standard and so

The judge should be able to touch the Stafford anywhere from the dog's nose to the tip of his tail.

the show ring is the test of successful breeding, although I still believe dog shows exclude important criteria such as health, intelligence and performance. To achieve these attributes as well as looks, sensibly planned management of breeding is necessary, and breed club shows must not be reduced to circuses for the exhibition of animals only. Nevertheless, many experts will agree that dog shows play an essential role in the assessment of a breed.

In England, large dog shows have a worthwhile and positive function. However, this may not appear the case to an observer at a Continental show, where very few specialist judges in the ring have taken the trouble to get to know the breed well in its country of origin, and judges who have never seen a Stafford in England attempt to instruct new judges and influence decisions concerning appointments. Such behaviour does not help the small number of Stafford owners and this relatively new breed on the Continent. There is no doubt that, as the popularity of the Stafford increases on the Continent, the exhibitors will demand better judges in the ring.

SHOW PRESENTATION
As with most things in life, the correct presentation of the Stafford has to be learnt: a judge can only judge a dog

Pulling upright on the lead encourages your Stafford to fix his head and hold the correct show pose.

In some countries, stacking is practised, where the dog is placed in position.

from what he can see. The dog has to learn to stand still on command and 'show itself off' and it must be moved at the correct speed. Only then does the judge get a true picture of the dog.

Joseph Dunn, among other tips for exhibitors, is insistent that no dog which is excitable and barks and snaps at the other entrants can be expected to win. He rightly says that such behaviour shows bad manners and bad training, when other exhibitors have made the effort to train their dogs to show themselves well. An unruly dog will not convince the judge how brave it is – the show ring is no place for aggression. A dog show is where one

expects to find a number of well-behaved dogs, which, along with their owners, should only display their best side.

Correct show training is essential, as the judge should be able to touch a dog anywhere from its nose to the tip of its tail. It is important to practise showing the dog's teeth and this training can be started when it is quite young. The dog must learn to stand patiently while its flews are raised so that the judge can determine the position of its teeth and also when its jaws are opened for its dentition to be checked. Playful practice at home will save excitement in the ring. Any dog

Meeting the Standard: Ch. Fernstaff Special Quest JW. Winner of seven CCs and four Reserve CCs, made into a Champion at 19 months.

that will not let itself be handled cannot be properly judged. It is best if a game of 'show time' is played at home. Perhaps a visitor can be asked to handle the dog, look at its teeth and watch it move.

THE CORRECT STANCE

The basic stance of the Stafford is important. The dog should be commanded to 'stand' and can be helped by an upward pull on the lead to fix the head, although I prefer to use small pieces of baked liver or cheese. From over thirty years' experience in the ring I have found the magic word 'treats' usually gets a dog in the right position. It is important when handling to keep the dog interested in the proceedings, and a piece of cheese, baked liver, dried fish or whatever the dog prefers is likely to work well. If the dog is a keen retriever then its favourite ball should be taken along, or a squeaky mouse might keep it alert.

In England 'stacking' is practised; I always admire the patience and pleasant nature of dogs when, foot by foot, they are put in their place, but I do not think they really look happy with this tiring routine of manipulation. Nor am I in favour of the form of presentation where the owner kneels behind the Stafford and pulls the lead upwards while the dog's

stomach or head is held up with the other hand. I think this looks very contrived, and I do not like to see it when I judge. A dog should be able to present itself under its own motivation.

SHOW MOVEMENT

Training a dog for shows should be undertaken several times a week but never for more than ten minutes at a time, in case it should tire and bore the dog. When moving the dog, it should not gallop but should move freely on the left-hand side of the handler. Faults can be camouflaged by careful positioning when standing a dog, but not when it is on the move, or with an experienced judge. It is up to the handler to present the dog at its best, but the dog can also be taught to make the best of itself. In every breed there are natural show dogs, described as 'show men' or 'show girls', whose innate ability takes them halfway to the top.

SHOW JUDGES

The internationally famous Bull Terrier 'Pope', Raymond Oppenheimer, put down his own thoughts on the requirements of a judge: "Mr Leo Wilson once gave, as his definition of a first-class judge, a man who never puts up a bad one. I would go further and say that he must also never leave a top-class dog out in the cold. For a judge to place at the top of the line a row of dogs of one particular type, some being very ordinary specimens of that type, and leave top-class specimens or other types without the proverbial sausage, just because they are not his types, is in my opinion to stamp him as a bad judge. What is more, such a judge will never for long be a successful breeder."

Staffords, like Bull Terriers, have both Terrier and Bulldog ancestry, therefore Raymond Oppenheimer's

strictures apply equally to Stafford judges.

An owner must appreciate that, to achieve success in the show ring, he or she must work closely with the breeder to attain the requirements of the Standard together; they will thus enjoy dog shows all the more. Such co-operation is evident in England where, unlike the Continent, very large entries show that, in the Stafford Bull Terrier clubs, the judges are accepted by the majority of the exhibitors.

Eng. Ir. Ch. Wyrefare Prince Naseem: Winner of 6 CCs and 6 Reserve CCs. Reserve Terrier Group Darlington Ch. Show 1999.

6 THE BREED STANDARDS

The Standard of the Breed describes an ideal animal, a breed goal, a combination of all the attributes in a perfect dog. Such a 'dream dog' will never exist, but it is a target for breeders. Without a Standard it is not possible to breed objectively, or to develop a uniform breed type in terms of temperament and other attributes.

The Stafford specialist John F. Gordon defines the Breed Standard as a picture created in words to illustrate what is demanded of the breed. This gives the breeder a goal at which to aim for the perfect dog. Of course there is no such thing as the perfect Staffordshire Bull Terrier. There are good, even exceptional, dogs, but there is always something bringing them up short of perfection.

THE 1935 STANDARD

Joseph Dunn wrote in *Our Dogs* that, after visiting a number of kennels belonging to some of the oldest and best-known breeders of Staffordshire Bull Terriers, he compiled, on April 26th 1935, a Breed Standard which he and the breeders agreed was typical of the breed. He included with his article a photograph of a two-and-a-half-year-old dog of the correct Stafford type. His measurements were: shoulder height 44.5 cm, head circumference 43 cm, neck 39 cm, chest 67 cm, length of back 41 cm, tail length 23 cm and weight 15 kg; he was kept in top-class condition and his ancestors could be traced back over thirty years. This model dog, the basis for the Breed Standard, was Jim the Dandy, who belonged to Jack Barnard and his brother.

Barnard himself commented that the desired breed type had originated from his dog, and this was then confirmed at the founding of the Staffordshire Bull Terrier Club; the picture preserves the historical authenticity of the breed. This ideal dog had quite a short back;

Jim the Dandy: the model for the Staffordshire Bull Terrier Breed Standard.

The dogs of 10 kg body weight were distinct Terrier types – others managed a proud 27 kg on the scales and these were obviously the descendants of the Bulldog in head and body.

At this time it was simply a sensible, diplomatic decision to create a Standard that would not directly exclude any of the breeders. Thus, the range of weights and sizes in the first Standard are a compromise which permitted agreement between the breeders. The tolerated weights ranged between 24-38 lbs (10.9 kg-17.3 kg); similarly the accepted height at the shoulder varied greatly between 15-18 ins (38.1-45.7 cm).

THE QUANDARY OF SIZE AND WEIGHT

Here we have arrived at one of the main problems in the breed. The inheritance of differences in size and weight has forced upon us a considerable amount of tolerance. As long as the breed exists there will always be excellent specimens of the Terrier type and the Bulldog type. The problems of weight and size have caused some heated arguments. The Bull Terrier Club has not had these problems because it has not included any weights or measurements in its Breed Standard from the start.

The Bull Terrier Standard refers to weight and size as follows:

the actual measurements show his back to be 3.5 cm shorter than his height at the shoulder, nearly ten per cent! He stood 17.5 ins (44.5 cm) at the shoulder which is greater than the subsequent 1948 top height limit of 16 ins (40.6 cm). Despite this, his weight of 15 kg was within today's desired range.

In other words, the original ideal dog was taller, lighter and squarer with a Terrier-type structure: today's dogs deviate somewhat from this. When the Breed Standard was under revision in 1948 there was a broad spectrum of dogs varying in weight and size. If we think back to the origin of the breed, body shape and size varied vastly between the Bulldog and the Terrier.

BREED VARIATIONS

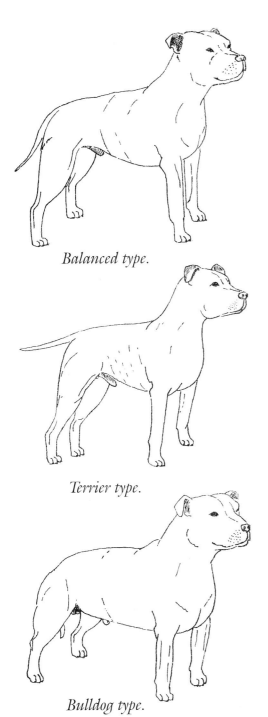

Balanced type.

Terrier type.

Bulldog type.

"There are neither weight nor height limits but there should be the impression of the maximum of substance relative to the size of the dog."

It is apparent that, after over a hundred years of breeding, dogs are neither too small nor too large, but an intermediate size has been maintained. Thus, a great deal of discussion and argument has been avoided.

There is little point in repeating the original Standard in this book. We can accept the word of Beilby, president of the Staffordshire Bull Terrier Club in 1950, who commented that the alterations made in 1948, following the recent revision of the Standard, showed little significant change from that written by the old-timers in 1935. W.M. Morley agreed with this statement but reminded us of the alterations to the weight and size limits.

The decision was taken to reduce the size of the Stafford from the original Standard of 1935 and to set the shoulder height at 5.1 cm lower, a drop from 45.7 cm to 40.6 cm. However, the weights remained the same as those in the Standard of 1935. Ultimately, such a change resulted in the dogs, between 1935 and 1948, gradually appearing heavier.

The experts agreed that this change produced a problem by discriminating against the excellent specimens of the larger type and there are Stafford fanciers today who still feel that the reduction in height in 1948 was wrong.

In fact, from 1949 to the present day the top dogs have often been above the requirements set down in the Standard for weight and height.

THE CURRENT BREED STANDARDS

The FCI (Fédération Cynologique Internationale) is the main organisation for dog breeds worldwide. It accepts the Breed Standards for each breed from its country of origin and, therefore, the Standard for the Staffordshire Bull Terrier is taken from the British Kennel Club.

In 1987 the Kennel Club revised all the Breed Standards, mainly in order to establish a model for all Standards, using certain basic terms and including some new formulations, or simply adding to or clarifying existing formulations.

The Staffordshire Bull Terrier Standard was only slightly changed from that written in 1948. These alterations are described and explained later in this chapter by Mary Pringle.

THE STAFFORDSHIRE BULL TERRIER BREED STANDARD, 1987

KC approved
FCI accepted, 24 June 1987

General appearance:
Smooth coated, well balanced, of great strength for his size. Muscular, active and agile.
Characteristics:
Traditionally of indomitable courage and tenacity. Highly intelligent and affectionate especially with children.
Temperament:
Bold, fearless and totally reliable.
Head and Skull:
Short, deep through with broad skull. Very pronounced cheek muscles, distinct stop, short foreface, nose black.
Eyes:
Dark preferred but may bear some relation to coat colour. Round, of medium size and set to look straight ahead. Eye rims dark.
Ears:
Rose or half pricked, not large or heavy. Full drop or pricked ears highly undesirable.
Mouth:
Lips tight and clean. Jaws strong, teeth large, with a perfect, regular and complete scissor bite, i.e. upper teeth closely overlapping the lower teeth and set square to the jaws.

Neck:
Muscular, rather short, clean in outline gradually widening towards shoulders.

Forequarters:
Legs straight and well boned, set rather wide apart, showing no weakness at the pasterns, from which point feet turn out a little. Shoulders well laid back with no looseness at elbow.

Body:
Close coupled, with level topline, wide front, deep brisket, well sprung ribs: muscular and well defined.

Hindquarters:
Well muscled, hocks well let down with stifles well bent. Legs parallel when viewed from behind.

Feet:
Well padded, strong and of medium size. Nails black in solid coloured dogs.

Tail:
Medium length, low set, tapering to a point and carried rather low. Should not curl much and may be likened to an old-fashioned pump handle.

Gait/Movement:
Free, powerful and agile with economy of effort. Legs moving parallel when viewed from front or rear. Discernible drive from hind legs.

Coat:
Smooth, short and close.

Colour:
Red, fawn, white, black or blue, or any one of these colours with white. Any shade of brindle or any shade of brindle with white. Black and tan or liver colour highly undesirable.

Size:
Weight: Dogs 28 lbs to 38 lbs. Bitches 24 lbs to 34 lbs. Desirable height (at withers) 14 to 16 inches, these heights being related to the weights.

Faults:
Any departure from the foregoing points should be considered a fault and the seriousness with which the fault should be regarded should be in exact proportion to its degree.

Note:
Male animals should have two apparently normal testicles fully descended into the scrotum.

Reproduced by kind permission of the Kennel Club.

At this point I wish to return to the far-reaching effects of the alteration to the Standard regarding weight and size. The 1987 version of the Standard dictates a suitable range for both weight and shoulder heights, the lower heights relating to the lower weights, etc. These limits resulted in some publications which systematically related shoulder heights and weights for both dogs and bitches. It is

Dogs		Bitches	
shoulder height	weight	shoulder height	weight
cm	*kg*	*cm*	*kg*
35.6	12.7	35.6	10.9
36.8	13.9	36.8	12.1
38.1	15.0	38.1	13.2
39.4	16.2	39.4	14.3
40.6	17.2	40.6	15.4

debatable whether it is a sensible idea to virtually employ slide rule measurements in this manner. Such a table has limited value, basically because of the variation between the Terrier type and the Bulldog type. To achieve a harmonious Terrier type we need a certain shoulder height which dictates a lighter dog than a Bulldog type of the same height.

We have already considered the subject of size and weight during the discussion of the 1935 Standard. It is quite likely that any reader comparing the size and weight of his dogs to those recommended in the table will find his animals to be somewhat heavier.

Some owners have an endearing ability to disregard the Standard when it does not suit the particulars of their breed, and with this kind of approach it is possible to live with size and height regulations. At shows, judges exercise a certain tolerance in such cases. Difficulties can arise where the Standards are followed and there is less tolerance. It would be better if a much clearer definition could be arrived at so that it could be understood internationally. At present, this lack of clarity does not help to improve the breed.

As the above table suggests, theory and fact are poles apart, and this is confirmed in the show ring. This is especially true of the Champion parades at breed club shows, where we see the best specimens.

COMMENTS ON THE BREED STANDARDS
by Mary Pringle
The original Breed Standard dates from 1935 when the breed was officially recognised by the English Kennel Club. In 1948 the Standard was amended and remained in operation until 1987.

In an endeavour to secure unification of all Breed Standards, the Kennel Club in 1987 issued a new

Breed Standard for the Staffordshire Bull Terrier. Naturally there were some adverse reactions. Fortunately there were not many significant changes.

The Kennel Club is the ruling body and judges are expected to judge to this current Standard. Some changes are merely in the wording, but the main changes are a reduction in description in the 'characteristics' clause of which we were so proud; the introduction of a new clause on 'movement' (gait) and an alteration to the 'faults' clause.

1. *General Appearance*
This is the first clause of the new Standard; it gives us the picture we must have in our minds of a Staffordshire Bull Terrier dog or bitch. It is a clear description: "smooth coated, well balanced, of great strength for his size. Muscular and agile."

2. *Characteristics*
The second clause concerning the characteristics of the breed has sadly been reduced and now reads: "Traditionally of indomitable courage and tenacity. Highly intelligent and affectionate especially with children." The words: "His off-duty quietness and trustworthy stability make him the foremost all purpose dog" have been omitted, which has displeased many of us.

3. *Temperament*
The third clause on temperament states: "Bold, fearless and totally reliable." These features must be retained at all costs.

4. *Head and Skull*
The fourth clause describes the head and skull: "Short, deep through with broad skull. Very pronounced cheek muscles, distinct stop, short foreface, nose black." The description of the head given by many of the old-timers in the breed was 'wedge-shaped' both when viewed from above and from the side. The ratio from nose to stop (which is the sudden drop below the eyes to the short foreface) and from stop to occiput is usually given as 1:3 to 2:3. When fully developed, a Stafford has a slight channel called a 'cleft' running down from the occiput and between the eyes to the stop. Muscle should be visible each side of the cleft on the top of the head, above the eyes and across in front of the eyes. Cheek muscles should be well developed: they are referred to as 'cheek bumps'. By two years old they should show up well. Heads may continue to mature up to three years old, especially in the male animal.

The head is a very distinctive part of the Stafford. Much importance should be given to it and, because the animal was developed originally for fighting,

Correct head type.

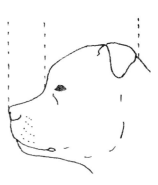

Correct head proportions.

Incorrect: Too fine a muzzle.

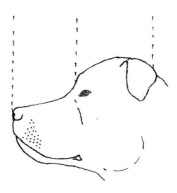

Incorrect: Shallow stop.

Incorrect head proportions.

Head study of Wardrum Geronimo, showing the distinctive proportions between muzzle and occiput, and the 'cheek bumps'.

the strong, large teeth, the broad skull and the cheek muscles are vital. It is the cheek muscles which help to give the strong appearance of the head. The bone structure of the skull should not be overdone, otherwise it will lead to whelping difficulties if there is exaggeration.

5. *Eyes*

The fifth clause concerns eyes: "Dark preferred but may bear some relation to coat colour. Round, of medium size and set to look straight ahead. Eye rims dark." The eyes should not be set too wide apart so as to spoil the expression and must not protrude.

6. *Ears*

The sixth clause describes ears: "Rose or half pricked, not large or heavy. Full drop or pricked ears highly undesirable." Little more needs to be said except that the whole expression is affected by the ear carriage. Ears of the type which 'fly off' at the side of the head are untidy and unattractive.

Incorrect: Ears too large.

Incorrect: Button ears.

Incorrect: Prick ears.

Incorrect: Ears set too low.

Correct: Rose ears.

7. *Mouth*

The seventh clause regarding the mouth is quite straightforward: "Lips tight and clean. Jaws strong, teeth large with a perfect regular and complete scissor bite, i.e. upper teeth closely overlapping the lower teeth and set square to the jaws."

115

DENTITION

Correct:
Scissor bite.

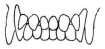

Side view of
scissor bite.

Incorrect:
Level bite.

Incorrect:
Undershot.

Incorrect:
Overshot.

8. *Neck*

The eighth clause describes the neck well: "Muscular, rather short, clean in outline gradually widening towards shoulders." It makes no reference to a distinct muscular arch from the occiput to the end of the neckline, referred to as the 'crest' which is seen when a male Stafford is alert.

9. *Forequarters*

The ninth clause describes the forequarters: "Legs straight and well boned, set rather wide apart, showing no weakness at the pasterns, from which point feet turn out a little. Shoulders well laid back with no looseness at elbow." While the legs are required to be set rather wide apart this does not mean there should be exaggeration. A 'Bulldog' front is not wanted. The shoulders should be clean, there should be no bulges or over-musculation. Ideally the shoulder blades should be well laid back, which is not altogether easy to obtain in an animal of the build of the Stafford. Certainly they must not be too perpendicular, or good movement will be affected and a clean sweep of the neck into the body will not be achieved.

A Stafford should 'stand up well on his pasterns' and the feet should only turn out a little. This 'turn-out' is supposed to help to distribute the

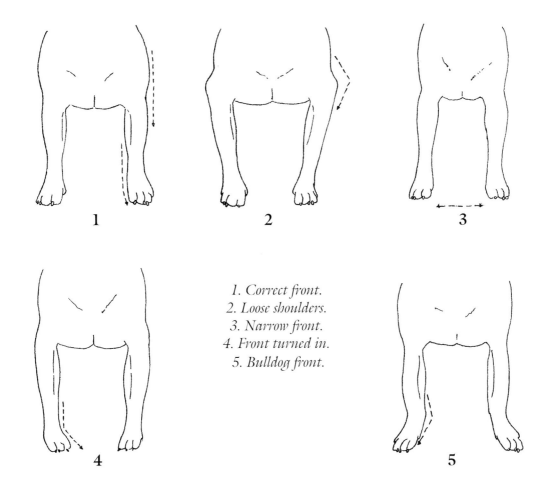

1. Correct front.
2. Loose shoulders.
3. Narrow front.
4. Front turned in.
5. Bulldog front.

weight of the strong chest and forequarters. No mention is made of the dewclaws which remain on the front legs, but if any appeared on the back legs they would be removed. Stud dogs make good use of their front dew claws when mating and they were not removed in the days of fighting dogs.

10. *Body*
The tenth clause describes the body: "Close coupled with level topline, wide front, deep brisket, well sprung ribs; muscular and well defined." A powerful compact dog is required, with a strong back which does not dip behind the shoulders. The topline should be level, then at the loin there will be a very slight rise, not a big

117

TOPLINE

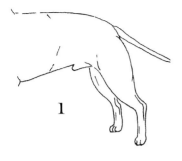

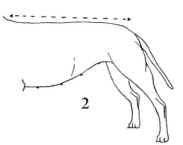

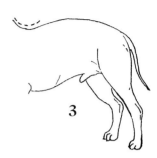

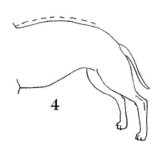

1. Correct back.
2. Long in back.
3. Sunken withers.
4. Roach back.
5. Sloping back and croup.

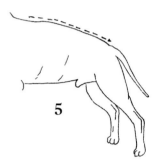

UNDERLINE

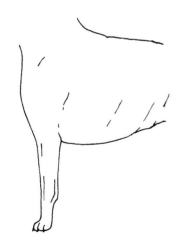

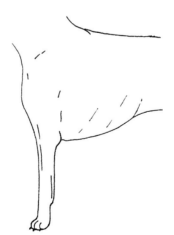

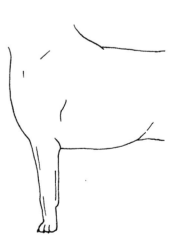

Correct underline.

Updrawn underline.

Underline too deep.

roach (a convex arching of the spine).
Nor should the back sway or drop in
the middle section, nor fall away to a
sloping croup. The loins should be
light and the coupling between the last
rib and the hip joints should be
compact, not long.

The front between the legs should
be wide so that there is plenty of space
for the lungs in the chest. The brisket
should be deep and the ribs well
sprung, giving room for both the
lungs and the heart to work well. An
imaginary line drawn from the bottom
of the chest should pass through the
point of the elbows on the legs.

There should be no belly on a fit dog.

11. *Hindquarters*
The eleventh clause describes the
hindquarters: "Well muscled, hocks
well let down with stifles well bent.

HINDQUARTERS

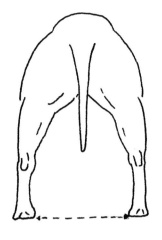

*Incorrect:
Standing
too wide.*

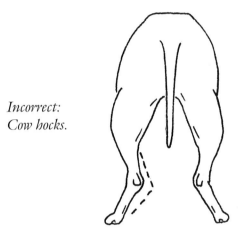

*Incorrect:
Cow hocks.*

Correct stance.

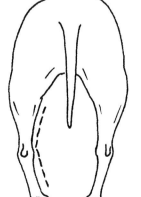

*Incorrect:
Turned in.*

119

Legs parallel when viewed from behind." There should be no exaggeration by hocks being too high or too low. Although stifles should be well bent, there should not be over-angulation nor too much length and the second thighs should be well developed. The legs must not be cow hocked, nor toed-in, but should be parallel when viewed from behind the dog.

12. *Feet*

The twelfth clause is concerned with the feet: "Well padded, strong and of medium size. Nails should be black in solid coloured dogs." The toes should be held closely together and the feet in balance with the size of the dog. The Stafford was bred to fight and had to move with agility so the pads should be strong and springy.

13. *Tail*

The thirteenth clause describes the tail: "Medium length, low set, tapering to a point and carried rather low. Should not curl much and may be likened to an old-fashioned pump handle." The root of the tail should be strong and should then taper off. It should not curl over the back nor be set too high and carried in a gay manner. Nor should it be set too low (as in dogs which fall away badly at the croup). It should be remembered that any dog

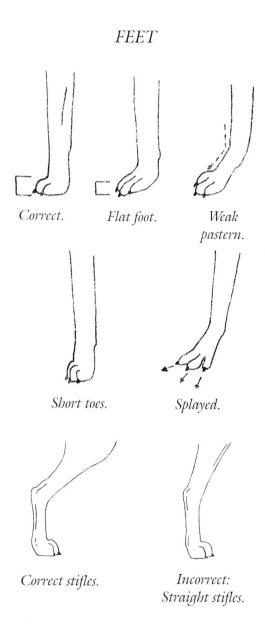

FEET

Correct.   *Flat foot.*   *Weak pastern.*

Short toes.   *Splayed.*

Correct stifles.   *Incorrect: Straight stifles.*

with courage will inevitably raise its tail when challenged by another.

It is said that the Stafford's tail needed to be strong, for a fighting dog could sometimes thump down on the floor with its tail in order to

120

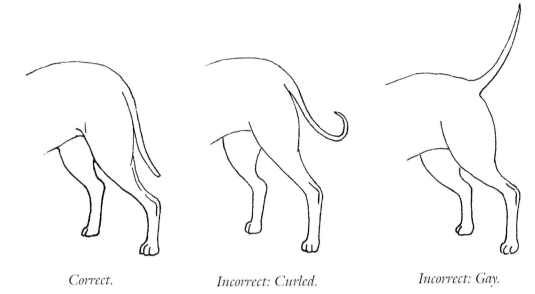

Correct.   *Incorrect: Curled.*   *Incorrect: Gay.*

manoeuvre itself into a better position.

14. *Gait/Movement*
The fourteenth clause describes gait or movement: "Free, powerful and agile with economy of effort. Legs moving parallel when viewed from front or rear. Discernible drive from the hind legs." This covers most things and a dog looking its height, moving freely and proudly, looks well.

15. *Coat*
The fifteenth clause describes the coat: "Smooth, short and close." In good condition, a Stafford's coat should shine, be of medium texture – neither silky nor coarse. It should be very pleasant to the touch.

16. *Colour*
The sixteenth clause concerns colour: "Red, fawn, white, black or blue or any one of these colours with white. Any shade of brindle or any shade of brindle with white. Black and tan or liver colour highly undesirable." Quite clear. Blue is rare and unless of a real grey shade with good pigmentation it is not desirable.

17. *Size*
The seventeenth clause concerns size: "Weight: dogs 28 lbs to 38 lbs. Bitches, 24 lbs to 34 lbs. Desirable height (at withers) 14 to 16 inches, these heights being related to weights." It is not easy to obtain the desired weight and height as stated, especially in mature animals. Young

animals will often be just within the Standard, but with maturity both the sexes usually finish up weighing more than the stated desired weight.

18. *Faults*

The present 'faults' clause has been reduced and now merely states: "Any departure from the foregoing points should be considered a fault and the seriousness with which the fault should be regarded should be in exact proportion to its degree."

The Standard states that male animals should have two apparently normal testicles fully descended into the scrotum.

The Breed Standard is a guide for both breeder and judges. In order to retain breed type and soundness, both must try to breed and to judge as near to the Standard as they can.

THE TRUE STAFFORD

Dog-fighting has been illegal for many, many years and, while Staffordshire

Ch. Rendorn Deadly Nightshade: A fine example of a Stafford that conforms closely to the Breed Standard.

The stamp of quality: Ch. Bombstaff Blackthorn At Bullhawk, owned by Sharon Pearce and bred by Russell Marsh.

Bull Terriers look aggressive and can behave so towards each other and towards the rest of the canine race, today's Stafford is a family dog. It is a special dog, not meant to be owned by fools. It is at its best living in the house, where it will play happily with children, curl up beside its owner on the settee or chair, welcome friends but be a guard against enemies. There is no other dog like it and it has been known to lay down its life protecting its owner.

7 THE BACKGROUND TO SUCCESSFUL BREEDING

This book is not intended as a handbook for the successful breeding of Staffordshire Bull Terriers but, as a specialist book concerned with a particular breed, it is appropriate to point out a number of peculiarities or special qualities which are of significance. A well-managed, planned kennel can be a fascinating hobby for dog owners. Those who consider it otherwise, such as a means of making quick money, will soon find themselves in difficulties.

THE BASIC REQUIREMENT

To become a successful kennel the basic requirement is for first-class animals. The recipe for success is a top-class bitch; I do not know of one successful kennel which began with a good male. Beware of self-deception; it is imperative that breeding stock is chosen meticulously – only the best is good enough for breeding. This

selection happens in the wild, where the survival of the fittest eliminates the sickly or the defective animal so that it never reaches a stage at which it could breed. Natural selection in the dog has been replaced with decisions made by breeders, often to the detriment of the breed. This kind of selective breeding must be undertaken with great care because of the effect it can have on the breed.

There is no excuse for using second-class dogs for breeding. A male which is never used at stud will not suffer in any way. Similarly, veterinary surgeons can provide no reasons why bitches should be any different, and they do not need to have puppies either. The widespread misconception that all bitches should have one litter is completely unfounded. Some people believe that it is important for a bitch to have puppies because rearing puppies will be a pleasure for her; and

Kecila Black Opal: When setting up your own kennel, the most important ingredient is a good bitch.

some families feel it is good to have a litter from the family pet so that their own children can learn about the facts of life.

Breeding for such reasons occurs in many breeds, including the Stafford, which we know is a good family pet, but it should be remembered that it is not easy for any breeder to find suitable homes for the puppies. From my many years of experience, I can say that it is many times more difficult to find good owners than it is to breed good dogs.

125

THE RESPONSIBILITIES OF BREEDING

Everyone who decides to breed has a moral responsibility towards the animals, which does not automatically end once the puppy is sold, and inappropriate breeding attracts impulse buyers from today's throwaway society. These impulse buyers are a great danger to our dogs: when the family goes on holiday the dog will end up in an animal home, or, worse, by the roadside.

Active breeding demands that a breeder be responsible for a puppy for the rest of its life. Unwanted Stafford puppies (and older dogs too) should not have to rely on animal homes or Staffordshire Bull Terrier Welfare Societies: they should always be taken back by the breeder.

After forty years of breeding, I realise how difficult it can sometimes be to acknowledge this responsibility, but anyone who has seen a well-reared puppy passed on to an irresponsible owner, where it vegetates in an unsuitable home, must recognise the problem. It is the duty of a breeder to help in such a situation, regardless of personal inconvenience. A puppy should not have to undergo such an experience, and all possibilities must be taken into consideration before breeding.

All responsible breeding begins with planning a good breeding programme. The following are essential: health, intelligence, aptitude, and, only then, looks. It is all very well to win prizes at dog shows but a breeder must be assured that, in the first instance, a dog is a reliable companion. Intelligence and aptitude are also necessary to cope with today's environment. If looks and the right anatomy are also present, then a dream has been realised, but the dream must follow in the right sequence: there are too many dumb and stupid show winners, Champions with hereditary defects.

PLANNING A BREEDING PROGRAMME

by Norman Berry

Breeding a litter is not a difficult exercise to carry out. Admittedly there are awkward matings, and problems can occur during the time of whelping, but, technically speaking, little knowledge is required to produce a litter.

Many thoughts on how to create and maintain a successful line of winning dogs have been put forward over the years and no doubt much of the writing on the subject has assisted our strains to develop.

There are many reasons for mating a bitch. One is the desire to breed a fine future prospect for the show ring. The rest of the litter must, of course, be sold off and there lies the danger of selling the wrong puppy. Therefore a wealth of knowledge of your stock by knowing the ancestors can be of great advantage when choosing your puppy. Money must not be allowed to take priority over your choice. Financial gain is the wrong incentive and should be put to one side – although it sometimes comes as a relief when veterinarian and feeding bills start to accumulate. If you breed good dogs there is no reason why you should not benefit from the surplus stock.

When a breeder has established a strong line, great interest can be aroused when watching the course of development through the animal's show career. I have enjoyed many happy moments watching dogs from our kennel winning at shows, and I can assure you financial gain is far from my thoughts, especially on the occasions when they receive first prizes and other acclamations.

There are many genuine breeders who care about their stock and their ultimate destination and lifestyle. They only breed one, or perhaps two, litters a year, not wishing to add to the ever-increasing number of unwanted dogs currently putting great strain on the rescue organisations. I believe restraint is the price to be paid for the popularity which encourages the interest of people outside the breed to take advantage of the opportunity to make financial gain at the expense of the breed. The objective of the true and dedicated breeder is to bring about an improvement in his stock. Essentially, he hopes to breed better stock than he already has, which may be at the end of its show days. In breeding a further litter, the hope is to retain virtues and improve deficiencies.

ESTABLISHING A STRONG LINE

Information is required if you are to establish a strong line. Questions must be asked, photographs perused and pedigrees studied. Gathering information takes time; people starting late in life need to absorb knowledge faster than younger people, although younger people may suffer from the early pressures of home-keeping etc. and may not have the time to spend on it that they might wish.

Genetic understanding, if not a fundamental grasp of the subject, can be an advantage although not a necessity. It can avoid wasting time on trying to achieve impossible goals.

Over the past thirty or forty years many good strains come to mind. One or two breeders carried out extensive breeding programmes and experimented quite rigidly with specific lines. I think of Jack Altoft of the well-known Goldwyns affix, his

127

Gochin Red Knight: Look carefully at other lines of Staffords in order to choose a good stud dog.

first mating being a bitch called Goldwyn. During the war, travelling was greatly restricted due to official regulations and it was quite difficult to achieve a mating with the chosen stud dog, Brindle Bill, a son of the founder of the 'M' line type of breeding, Brindle Mick. This mating to Goldwyn produced a dog puppy called Wheatley Lad. The mating was planned to be repeated but, unfortunately, Brindle Bill died, cutting off any chance of a repeat mating. The next best choice was Wheatley Lad's litter brother Sunny Bill; this union produced a further excellent litter from which a bitch was retained, Brindle Diana. Later she was put to Wheatley Lad, her uncle and half-brother. From this mating came Ch. Goldwyns Leading Lad. Due to this success, the mating was repeated and resulted in another Champion, Ch. Goldwyns Leading Lady. A further inbred experiment then took place by mating the two aforementioned animals and, you have guessed it, produced another flyer, Ch. Goldwyns Lucky Lad!

To summarise, the first inbred mating was a brother and sister experiment repeated, and then the brother and sister from each litter were put together. From two sib-matings, a further union was contrived and turned out a further success.

After searching through various pedigrees, I cannot find any breeding as close as Jack Altoft's programme. Although it proved successful for him and resulted in three Champions, I feel the results have highlighted the point that I am trying to emphasise – it could also have had disastrous consequences. The method employed reduced the gene pool considerably in favour of the breeder.

LINE BREEDING

Planning matings of closely related dogs is not always the answer to success. Certainly, without knowledge of ancestral dominance and traits, such matings could lead to repeated failures.

During the late 1940s to the late 1970s there was another ardent follower of line breeding, Bob Salisbury of South Elmsall, North Yorkshire. The consequences of his efforts were a great influence on what is now known as 'the Yorkshire Line'. From this breeding came two influential stud dogs, Ch. Black Tusker and Ch. Hurricane of Judael, and between them they have produced fourteen and seven English Champions respectively.

During the 1930s Bob Salisbury bred Bulldogs and Bullmastiffs.

Ch. Hurricane of Judael.

Rumbuster, a prominent dog in Bob Salisbury's breeding programme.

Having admired Staffords for many years, he finally succumbed to them by acquiring a bitch called Brigands Spitfire, a purchase from J. Dunn who was a leading figure during the early pioneering days of the Stafford in England. During the early 1950s Bob started to experiment with line breeding. Earlier he had Tenacious Pete, whose sire, Brindle Bill, as you may recall, was the foundation sire of Mr Altoft's breedings. Brindle Bill was mated to Beladdona Black Queen, thus producing Ch. Nita's Choice and a further bitch Elegant Girl; the latter was put to Ch. Quiz of Wyncroft resulting in Ch. Pal of Aveth.

During this time Bob formed a partnership with George Guest, the famous breeder of Ch. Nita's Choice. Subsequently, Ch. Nita's Choice was mated to Ch. Pal of Aveth and produced a bitch they registered as Good Brew. She was mated to Ch. Quiz of Wyncroft, from which a male puppy, Happy Larry, was retained and later put to a Bellerophen bitch and from this litter came Greybarn Humphrey.

At this point the breeding became

SETTING A TYPE
Three generations of Rendorn breeding

TOP LEFT:
Grandmother:
Rendorn Run Deep
(aged 11 years).

TOP RIGHT:
Mother: Rendorn
Rialto (5 years).

LEFT:
Son: Rendorn
Rule The Roust
(6 months).

more intense. Mating Humphrey to a litter sister, Dark Eyed Susan, resulted in a dog that was to figure quite prominently in Bob's breeding programme. This was Rumbuster, who was not shown very much, rather a short-legged brindle, a good type. His progeny figured quite prominently in the pedigrees of Ch. Black Tusker and Ch. Hurricane of Judael. This was achieved by mating Rumbuster to a daughter, Bellerophen Wonder Girl. She whelped Black King, the sire of Ch. Black Tusker and grandfather of Ch. Hurricane of Judael.

Quite a number of half-brother/sister matings took place involving Rumbuster, he himself being the product of a similar mating deriving from thoughtful line breeding, which was later to pay great dividends to the breed.

Rumbuster produced three Champions during his stud career, they being Ch. Regency Gal, a brindle bred by Bob, Ch. Monkhill Candy, a fawn, and Ch. Vesper Andromeda, a richer red.

I have found during the time I have been interested in the more serious side of dog breeding, and I make no excuses for my remarks, that many people do not commence their breeding programme with great seriousness, in so far as a certain amount of knowledge and experience

of the breed is essential to enter seriously on a programme intended to produce a successful strain of good sound type stock.

The objective of any would-be breeder hoping to achieve such reward should be to buy a good line-bred bitch who need not be a top winner herself but must be carrying in-depth line breeding to good, winning stock. Not all bitches produced by top kennels are good lookers. Winners at this level are still difficult to produce. Should she develop into a top-class specimen, this should be regarded as a bonus. No breeder can guarantee success with every sale and should a puppy not turn out a winner, all is not lost! Despair should not be allowed to take a hand but rather the next step is to select a suitable dog of the same line, or as near as possible to the immediate line.

Having had success with closely related dogs, for example, half-brother/sister matings, I feel this is the best and safest mating to advocate in our breed. Sister/brother matings and parent to offspring are, in my opinion, rather too close, for reasons I will dwell on later. Close breeding should only be practised if the breeder is clear in his own mind that he has come as close as possible to perfectly achieving his ideal animal. The disadvantage of such matings is

TRACING A LINE

Represented by Jim Beaufoy's Wyrefare kennel.

Sire:
Wyrefare
Midland
Sureshot.

Dam:
Fromestaff
Extravaganza
of Wyrefare.

Son: Ch. Wyrefare
Prince Naseem of
Wyrefare

Mincol The Governor: Sired by Ch. Wyrefare Prince Naseem
of Wyrefare out of Kecila Black Opal.

that, while finer virtues are being fixed, undesirable combinations of character are also being implanted and can be one hell of a job to eliminate. I am sure many people in Staffords would endorse my remarks that in our breed no kennel is far enough advanced to carry out such close matings as described, due to the diversity of pedigrees relating to the contemporary Staffordshire Bull Terrier. When only mediocre stock is available, in-breeding should not be considered.

IN-BREEDING

Most people consider in-breeding to be distasteful and undesirable but really it is one of the most natural functions of wild animal packs, as one would observe. In nature, incest is carried on on a grand scale, all gregarious animals being subjected to in-breeding as a matter of course. Usually the pack is taken over by one dominant male who then commences to mate all females over a number of years and when the time comes for him to be ousted from his privileged position in the pack, due to infirmity or old age, his place is taken over, quite likely by one of his many sons. He, in turn, starts to copulate with his own sisters. This is repeated over future generations and so on.

To be on safer ground, the method of line breeding (half-brother to half-sister or cousin to cousin) does give some latitude and allows the breeder to eliminate bad points that can arise when trying to establish a strain of his own. Unfortunately the disadvantage is the greater number of gene combinations that must be expected to occur in the puppies produced.

A thoughtless approach to the subject, possibly resulting in a mismatch which can be reflected in future generations, cannot be condoned. The odd chance flyer may occur but is not often repeated. Should the said animal be a dog, it should not be regarded as a saviour of the breed, a view which no doubt would encourage people to rush out and use him. A poorly bred bitch is as unreliable as an ill-bred dog and even though they may have brought great success for their owners in the show ring, they are most unlikely to have been endowed with genetic power of any great strength and can hardly be expected to continuously produce good specimens.

THE PREPOTENT DOG

Occasionally, a prepotent dog arrives on the scene who seems to have the ability to produce excellent specimens to various types of bitches. This particular dog quickly becomes extremely popular and is used quite extensively. Encouraged breeders, having learned of his prepotent strength, hope that he may enhance their luck in producing a good litter. Having been successful, the clever ones keep in line of the prepotent sire and go on to further success and establish a breeding pattern of their own.

I expect there will always be people who cannot see or appreciate a good thing when they have it stuck under their noses and, for reasons best known to themselves, go off and use the next popular dog that takes their fancy, disregarding the fact that they have ignored the opportunity offered to them to advance their breeding programme. Over the past ten years, I can think of three of four of these prolific dogs that have certainly left their mark on the breed, their owners having used a good dog with double genetic strength (homozygous qualities) and carrying all the virtues they obviously desired. One would surmise this was the reason for using the dog in the first place.

Such a dog as previously described should be used as a point to build from. In doing so it will prove that more favourable results will occur. It cannot be emphasised too strongly that a kennel basing its programme on inferior breeding stock is handicapping itself so severely as to allow nothing more than limited success. Most

Stafford kennels are limited to no more than two or three breeding bitches. Therefore it is most important that they carry the greatest virtues in double strength and their pedigrees be of the highest possible order in a great depth of homogosity for the strain.

BREEDING BACK
The method of breeding back to some well-known illustrious sire or dam is considered and recommended by some breeders. It may have its rewards but one should consider the amount of time and trouble involved even if it is successful. I consider this method a rather roundabout way of arriving at a hopeful conclusion when one considers the possible combination of genes to conjure with when breeding back over generations: the genetic pool becomes immensely unpredictable, especially if somewhere along the way there have been a couple of out-crosses. Considering most Stafford pedigrees this is almost inevitable – the thought makes the mind boggle. To follow this line of thought, when one considers the distance and diversity of the individual pedigrees, this method is nothing more than a euphemism for out-crossing!

OUT-CROSSING
The method of out-crossing is more or

less self-explanatory. After looking through the results of show catalogues, it can be seen that in some cases this does bring immediate results, either through ignorance or by a calculated chance mating of two good-looking specimens from two different lines. The fact still remains that one must expect the results of the second generation to vary quite enormously. By employing a line breeding exercise, one can again bring back stability. Great care should be exercised in selecting out-cross matings. One should ensure that as few recessive traits as possible are introduced. One way to proceed is to choose a dog which possesses the desired quality, is related as nearly as possible, and has similar genetic make-up to the other character. Be prepared for the possible occurrence of an out-cross, and its attendant problems. The message is quite clear. Keeping pedigrees as tight as possible and considering only the first three

generations of the two pedigrees, thirty dogs carrying all the virtues and faults have been employed. Any further back and the task seems to be getting more difficult and diverse and, in my opinion, of purely historic interest only.

BLOODLINES

H.N. Beilby, a pioneer of the breed, analysed in his book, published in 1943, the registrations between May 1935 and December 1937; there were 580. Then he broadened his investigation to cover all registrations up to the end of 1943. His analysis revealed four male bloodlines as dominant in the breed. The descendants of the four bloodlines each had their own common ancestor, which enabled the different bloodlines to be distinguished from each other. Beilby's analysis resulted in the picture shown in the following table: many of today's breeders try to trace their lines back to 1944 and these dogs.

Bloodline	Ancestor	Descendants
J	Fearless Joe	300
L	Game Lad	120
M	Brindle Mick	300
B	Rum Bottle	100 (Westall Strain)

Beilby was obviously influenced by the genetic research of the thoroughbred horse-breeder, Rosslyn Bruce, who wrote the foreword to this book. Beilby correctly emphasises the importance of a good brood bitch, describing them as founders of 'the families'. In his analysis of dog breeding, Beilby drew parallels with Rosslyn Bruce's theories, in particular by demonstrating 'tap root' bitches to be of great importance. The term 'tap root' describes dams who, over many generations, form the bottom line of the pedigrees: i.e. the daughters are kept and then subsequently bred from and one of their daughter is kept, and so on. It is an old theory, taken from breeders of thoroughbred horses, which credits dams with the ability to pass on their characteristics to their descendants, although there has never been any established proof.

For today's breeder these deliberations are only of academic interest: it is rather sad that Beilby's ideas have never been tried with the Stafford. To follow them through, a long-term planned approach needs to be undertaken by breeders with large kennels, like Raymond Oppenheimer's Ormandy Bull Terrier kennels, and there have been no such major breeders of Staffordshire Bull Terriers. A quick reference to today's Stafford reveals no such lines or families.

Beilby's analysis of the breed situation at the end of 1943 is interesting. In his opinion the goal of breeders should be:
1. To eliminate the undershot mouth by careful selection of stock, avoiding lines or families with the fault.
2. To breed for better movement and correct hind leg angulation. Beilby regarded good, sound movement as an indication of a healthy dog. The Kennel Club included a clause on movement in the 1987 revised Breed Standard.
3. To eliminate broad, flat feet and weak pasterns.

BREED TYPE
I have discussed difference in type between earlier Bulldogs and Terriers elsewhere in this book. These differences are still visible today. Denise Eltinge says of this difference in type that, occasionally, judges and breeders of other breeds deny a particular type the recognition it deserves because they do not appreciate these variations in the Stafford. Such a variation in type does not occur in most of the other Terrier breeds, where uniformity of type has been achieved.

Denise Eltinge is perfectly correct in emphasising that "in some Staffords a definite type stands out, and if there were not a tolerance in the breed towards variety, then breeding Staffords would not be so fascinating; perhaps more important, an aspect of the character and nature of the breed would be lost." Following on from that, she worked out certain breed characteristics which appear in today's Staffords and go back to their ancestors.

The basic difficulty with the Stafford is that features inherited from both Bulldogs and Terriers are not easy to

Bulldog Characteristics

Desirable	*Undesirable*
Small, low-set, rose ears	Undershot teeth
Short foreface	Elbow turn-out
Ample bone	Weak pastern
Large, upturned nose	Loose shoulder assembly
Driving movement	Lippiness
Deep, wide skull	Splayed feet
Out-turn of front feet	Short legs
Deep brisket	Short or screw tail
Broad chest	Loose or heavily wrinkled skin
Pronounced cheek muscles	Roach back
Round, widely-set eyes	

Terrier Characteristics

Desirable	*Undesirable*
Clean, tight lip line	Full prick or high-set ears
Level topline	Long, snipey muzzle
Strong, upright pasterns	Long foreface
Straight front leg	Lack of a distinct stop
Tidy, attractive feet	Shallow depth of skull
Pump handle tail	Narrow skull
Scissor bite	Small nose
Parallel movement	Almond eyes
	Closely-set eyes
	Light bone
	Stiff hindquarter movement
	Lack of rib spring (slab sided)

Breeding Staffords must be regarded as a highly specialised business.

mix and achieve an ideal anatomical combination. It is difficult to separate the gene combinations which arose early in the breed, and therefore it is difficult to separate the intimately associated desirable and undesirable qualities. This is the principal reason why many faults are so difficult to eradicate. Fifty years of planned breeding and following of a Standard has obviously not been enough to attain a uniform breed, although other Terrier breeds have reached that goal.

It is, I think, very important that Stafford breeders should understand their breed's connection with Bulldogs and Terriers. A balanced breed is required, a Stafford which is not too similar to the Terrier or the Bulldog; the ideal type lies somewhere in the middle.

A SELECT BREEDING STUDY
Denise Eltinge shall end the chapter: "Breeding Staffordshire Bull Terriers is not a hobby for those seeking a little weekend diversion; serious ethical and humanitarian responsibilities accompany the work and expense.

"No-one should begin a breeding kennel without specialist knowledge and a clear understanding of the terms 'phenotype' and 'genotype'; and the priorities must be health, intelligence, aptitude and then, and only then, looks."

8 THE FUTURE OF THE BREED

The popularity of the Stafford in its country of origin, England, must surely be a healthy indication of the future for this breed. Staffords have an extremely large gene pool and the dangers associated with overbreeding are neither likely nor apparent. They are impressive dogs with exceptional characters, and are undemanding and easy to look after, well suited to family life.

SENSIBLE BREEDING

The great popularity of the Stafford has attracted, on the whole, sensible breeders, not those who only wish to make a quick profit. Its widespread distribution throughout the country makes it possible for anyone to buy a young Stafford at a reasonable price. Another reason for the remarkably responsible breeders may be that the interest in the Stafford abroad has been much less than for other breeds. In those breeds which are popular

overseas, the unrealistic, fantasy prices have completely turned breeders' heads, whereas the limited export of Staffords to the Continent has not seriously affected their price at home.

CONTINENTAL DEVELOPMENT

Much the same low-key development of the breed has been taking place in other countries, where the Stafford has been gaining new friends. There have been few difficulties, except for the occasional wrong decision arising from insufficient contact with England and inaction on the part of the breed clubs. In 1988, a sensible new approach released the Stafford club from the guardianship of others whose interests were mainly in their own breeds. It should now be possible to combine the efforts of all relevant active bodies so that personal interests are second to the common goal, and then the quality of the breed on the Continent will improve, which should bring the

The qualities of the Stafford have made the breed popular overseas. This is Bullhawk Affinity, bred by Sharon Pearce.

Stafford many new friends.

German registration figures for Staffords in 1987 show them to be twice those of previous years, indicative of the increasing interest in the Staffordshire Bull Terrier. The 'all-purpose' has a lot to offer and during the last few years there has been increased interest in the breed. Slowly, its characteristics and special qualities are becoming discovered in Germany. German Stafford fanciers should not, however, become complacent; there is still a long way to go before the Stafford achieves the popularity it enjoys in England. This should not discourage but rather act as an incentive, as should the evidence of the Standard Bull Terrier having held its own in Germany for the last twenty years. One thing must be clear: both breeds have much in common. Many people who have chosen the Bull Terrier did so because of its incredible character; the Stafford is exactly the same except it is lodged in a smaller, more compact, modified frame.

It is certainly not easy to accustom dog lovers who are used to the shapes of their native dogs to the external appearance of an imported breed. However, all that is needed is time. I can vouch for this because I have done pioneer work for twenty-five years in order to accustom a very large number of people to the appearance of the Staffordshire Bull Terrier which they find strange at first sight.

PROMOTION THROUGH SHOWING

The popularity of the breed depends largely on Stafford owners and friends and their efforts to show them off on every possible occasion. The club show with hand-picked English judges is invaluable for the further development of the breed, and yet it is just as important to exhibit the Stafford at large international shows and before the general public. Take note of the huge number of spectators at a European Championship show, compared with an ordinary, well-run speciality show, and the impact of promotion through showing can be appreciated. Stafford breeders and owners must make their presence felt at these large shows.

The breeder Ingo Pruss did not shy away from the effort and cost, and he even entered progeny classes, in which the Staffords had to overcome some handicaps. It is essential for Staffords

The future of the Stafford lies in the hands of responsible breeders.

to be present on these big occasions; they are as important as the breed club shows where each dog can be assessed by a knowledgeable specialist judge, and they give an opportunity to Stafford owners in Germany to meet other dog lovers and discuss their dogs, so that the breed can be shown off to anyone interested. Too often the Stafford benches are empty as clever exhibitors avoid the tiresome waiting around that is involved, but this is very poor public relations. Thousands of dog lovers come to these shows to see and learn about different breeds, and the genuine Stafford supporter should be in his place by the dog's bench where he can talk to and answer the questions of people who are interested in the breed. This applies to international shows anywhere where the Stafford is not well known.

The German Staffordshire Bull Terrier Club has made good international public relations its goal. There are many people outside the UK who would be interested in a good dog, but they have to be told about the breed. That is the aim of this book. I have written it because there is a need for it, not for financial considerations. It could be the introduction to the breed for many dog lovers who only need just such a book to focus their interest. All breeders and Staffordshire Bull Terrier owners should find it a useful and handy book, not only for themselves, but also for the interested dog lover who wants to know more about this all-purpose dog.

Outside England, there is much work to be done to promote the Stafford – a great challenge that brings its own reward with ownership of one of the best of dogs, perfect for today's environment. They deserve a place up among the other breeds.